THE WORLD'S CLASSICS

THE PROSE POEMS
AND LA FANFARLO

CHARLES BAUDELAIRE was born in Paris in 1821. His father died when Baudelaire was 5 and his mother's remarriage in 1828 had a traumatic effect on his character. In 1841 his stepfather sent him on a voyage, that was meant to take him to Calcutta, but the homesick and rebellious Baudelaire insisted on leaving the ship after visiting Réunion and Mauritius and returned to France. In the following year he inherited 100,000 francs, which he proceeded to spend with such speed that his family appointed a lawyer to manage his fortune. Constantly in debt, Baudelaire's life became one of poverty, disorder, and squalor. In 1860 he suffered a minor stroke, probably as a result of syphilis. Four years later he moved to Belgium, in the vain hope of restoring his fortune and establishing his fame. In 1866 he suffered a series of strokes, leading to paralysis and aphasia, and was brought back to Paris where he died in August 1867. Baudelaire is best known for his collection of verse poetry, *The Flowers of Evil*, which was first published in 1857, and which led to his being found guilty of outraging public decency. Forced to suppress six of the poems, Baudelaire revised and enlarged the collection and republished it in 1861. His other works include studies of intoxicants and essays on caricature. He was a perceptive critic of contemporary art and literature, and a sensitive translator and adaptor of Edgar Allan Poe and Thomas de Quincey.

ROSEMARY LLOYD's books include *The Land of Lost Content: Children and Childhood in Nineteenth-Century France* (1992). She has translated George Sand's *The Master Pipers* (World's Classics).

THE WORLD'S CLASSICS

CHARLES BAUDELAIRE

The Prose Poems and La Fanfarlo

Translated with an Introduction by
ROSEMARY LLOYD

Oxford   New York
OXFORD UNIVERSITY PRESS

Oxford University Press, Great Clarendon Street, Oxford OX2 6DP

Oxford New York

Athens Auckland Bangkok Bogota Bombay
Buenos Aires Calcutta Cape Town Dar es Salaam
Delhi Florence Hong Kong Istanbul Karachi
Kuala Lumpur Madras Madrid Melbourne
Mexico City Nairobi Paris Singapore
Taipei Tokyo Toronto

and associated companies in
Berlin Ibadan

Oxford is a trade mark of Oxford University Press

Translation and editorial material © Rosemary Lloyd 1991

First published as a World's Classics paperback 1991

British Library Cataloguing in Publication Data
Data available

Library of Congress Cataloging in Publication Data
Baudelaire, Charles, 1821-1867.
[Poems. English. Selections]
The prose poems and La Fanfarlo/Charles Baudelaire, translated
with an introduction by Rosemary Lloyd.
p. cm.- (The World's classics)
Includes bibliographical references.
1. Baudelaire, Charles, 1821-1867—Translation, English.
I. Lloyd, Rosemary. II. Baudelaire, Charles, 1821-1867. Fanfarlo,
1991. III. Title. IV. Series.
PQ2191.A244 1991 841'.8—dc20 90-44124
ISBN 0-19-282703-0

3 5 7 9 10 8 6 4

Printed in Great Britain by
BPC Paperbacks Ltd.
Aylesbury, Bucks

CONTENTS

INTRODUCTION

That Baudelaire was one of the world's greatest poets is beyond dispute: but to consider him solely as the author of *The Flowers of Evil* is to ignore not only the intellectual perception and the passionate enthusiasm of his art and literary criticism, but also the ambitious experimentation or playful pastiche that inspires his creative prose writing. Living in the golden age of the French novel, he longed, from an early stage, to make his mark in that genre. With a characteristic blend of optimism, aesthetic conviction, and monetary wishful thinking, he announced to his mother, in a letter of 1847, the following New Year's resolution:

From the beginning of next year, I'm turning to a new trade—by which I mean the creation of works of pure imagination,—the Novel. I do not need to demonstrate to you here how grave, beautiful, and infinite this particular art is. As we are discussing material matters, all you need to know is that *good or bad, everything can be sold*: it's just a question of assiduity.

His critical writing reveals a determination both to understand the mechanisms used by novelists and short-story writers, and, typically, to make better use of those same mechanisms. But while his ambitions were boundless, the pragmatic difficulties of completing a full-scale novel seem to have been beyond him, partly for practical reasons associated with the chaotic and often sordid life-style his financial position forced him to adopt, and partly, there can be no doubt, because of his own temperament. Nevertheless, if his ambitions foundered where the novel was concerned, he still continued, throughout his creative life, to experiment with the possibilities of prose. His creative and critical writing, his prose and his poetry are linked together by a complex network of cross references.

In the years immediately preceding the 1848 revolution, years of turmoil both for Baudelaire and for France, he, like Samuel Cramer, the hero of *La Fanfarlo*, began to establish a reputation based more on potential than on production. Nevertheless, he did publish several brief prose pieces in addition to *La Fanfarlo* itself, anecdotal and journalistic responses to Balzac's huge productivity or to the many guides to beginners that flourished at the time. 'How to pay your debts when you're a genius', published in November 1845, is a punning and tongue-in-cheek account of how the great architect of *The Human Comedy*, faced with the need to repay on the following day a debt of 12,000 francs, sells (in advance) two articles to leading newspapers, then commissions friends to write these articles for him. In 'Advice to Young Writers', published in 1846, he offers a flippant and cynical series of suggestions, of which the following is typical: 'as for those who are giving themselves to poetry, or have already successfully done so, my advice to them is never to abandon it. Poetry is one of the arts that bring in most money.' Both these articles have points in common, thematically as well as stylistically, with *La Fanfarlo*, the extended short story he published in 1847, around the time when he was first coming into contact with Edgar Allan Poe. The power of Poe's imagination, the importance he placed on intellect rather than inspiration in creating the work of art, and his insistence that a short-story writer must reject all extraneous material and aim to produce a totally unified piece all greatly influenced the young poet. Yet *La Fanfarlo* obviously has less to do with Poe's supernatural than with the ironic, frequently self-mocking, tales of his earlier models, the French poet Gautier, to whom he dedicated *The Flowers of Evil*, and the German Romantic writer Hoffmann, whose influence can be seen particularly in Baudelaire's studies of laughter and the comic. The writer whose influence is most evident here, however, is Balzac, and critics have suggested various parallels, on the one hand, between Samuel Cramer and such Balzacian heroes as Rastignac and Rubempré, and on the other hand, between the major themes and those of *Béatrix*. Baudelaire himself, in a footnote in the text, refers the readers to Balzac's intense, erotic short story 'The Girl with the Golden Eyes', the dedication of which to the painter Delacroix, whom Baudelaire much admired, would not have escaped his notice. Nevertheless, *La Fanfarlo* is interesting less as a testimony to other exponents of the art, than as an indication of the young Baudelaire's half-cynical, half-fascinated assessment of the interrelationship of passion and aesthetics, of his delight in the unexpected and the antithetical, and of his ability to produce a prose style which moves easily between irony and enthusiasm, mockery and sympathy.

His analysis of Samuel Cramer, part parody of the typical aspiring poet, part unflinching self-analysis, focuses on dichotomies: between aspiration and achievement, between the delicacy of Cramer's poetics and the crudeness of his pragmatics, between romantic love and sexual desire. Above all, it constantly overturns expectations, revealing the poet's materialistic hedonism, and the ease with which the wronged wife manipulates her revenge, and allowing both sexual success and artistic fame to fall, not to the hero, but to the women.

In *La Fanfarlo* Baudelaire celebrates the modern dancer, preparing the ground for Mallarmé's subtle, complex evaluations of the ballet by his earthier appreciation of a combination of spontaneity, vitality, and strength that translates poetry directly into physical form. But he also celebrates in her an equivalent of Samuel in terms of her appreciation of the setting and preliminaries for passion, developing, in the clothes she wears, the furnishing of her house, and the meals she provides, the kinds of correspondences between inner and outer worlds, public and private domains, that he explores throughout his writing, and that reappear particularly in the prose poems.

The character of Mme de Cosmelly shows Baudelaire giving surprisingly sympathetic treatment to a type whom we might have expected him to approach with more irony. The innocent girl, married to the first man who presents himself and betrayed shortly after, becomes, in Baudelaire's hands, not the stock figure of melodrama, but a vehicle for a subtle exploration both of the intensity of awakened desire in a respectable, conventionally educated young woman, and of the case with which her apparent naïvety allows her to exploit Samuel's predatory intentions without falling victim to them.

A story of considerable wit and lightness of touch, spiced with perceptive comments on ballet and the art of furnishing, and refreshingly sharp in its presentation of its three major characters, *La Fanfarlo* deserves to be better known. Neverthe-less, it clearly did not set Baudelaire the degree of stylistic challenge that most stimulated him: he himself once remarked, to justify his use of the sonnet, that because of the constraints imposed by the form, the idea burst forth all the more intensely. The challenge of prose poetry, however, manifests itself throughout his writing career. Just as, in his literary criticism, he inserts into his own analysis pastiches or parodies of the writers under discussion, so from an early stage he explores the possibilities of a single theme in both verse and prose form. Such doublets can be found in the section of *The Flowers of Evil* entitled 'Le Vin' and his studies of wine and hashish, just as we find him reworking the theme of his beloved's hair in both 'La Chevelure' in *The Flowers of Evil* and 'A Hemisphere in a Head of Hair' in the *Short Prose Poems*, to give just two of the better known examples.

These are, moreover, no mere finger exercises, but part of Baudelaire's constant analysis of the well-springs of language and his determination to discover the means of expression best suited to conveying the nature of modern city life. Drawing on the poetic prose of such writers as Rousseau and Chateau-briand, and on the attempts of several nineteenth-century writers, particularly Aloysius Bertrand, to combine certain of the restrictions of poetic form with the freedom of prose, Baude-laire sought a form of language capable of conveying the complexity, the cacophony, and the unexpected juxtapositions of a large city such as Paris. Although not all of his prose poems are based in the capital. each of them reflects the mentality of an individual whose responses and emotions are forged, not by the countryside, as was the case with Rousseau and Chateau-briand, but by the city. (Even the exotic richness of the tropical paradise in 'Beautiful Dorothea' is set against Dorothea's image of a city whose riches and beauties are other but probably greater.) And whereas Bertrand's inspiration comes from an imaginative reconstruction of medieval Dijon, Baudelaire's is resolutely modern, confronting the Paris of Louis-Philippe and Napoléon III, the Paris that Haussmann's plans were transform-ing into the city we know today.

Baudelaire's focus on a large, modern city is both thematic and metaphorical or allegorical. The potential for isolation of the individual within the crowd, the availability of varied and inexpensive entertainments, the contrast between rich and poor, young and old, and the sheer incongruity of much human behaviour in an urban environment allow for the presentation of numerous portraits of men and women, either observed from a distance, when the imagination is free to create a context and a psychology for them, or from close up, when the narrator as friend or lover is forced to admit the inadequacy of the intellect to explain the complexities of human psyche. This discovery is itself embedded in one of the work's most celebrated analogies, that in which the poet claims that we see less looking through an open window than when we gaze from the street at a window across which the curtains are drawn. But the city provides not only the widows and the prostitutes, the lunatics, the beggars, and the pretentious philistines, it also offers images of the artist—the clowns and acrobats who seek to earn a precarious living entertaining a fickle public, the dogs who leap through hoops or the donkeys who continue with their tasks regardless of the city's hedonism, perhaps also the glazier who refuses to give his clients a rose-coloured view of life—and cameos of the child. Depictions of the artist as entertainer abound in nineteenth-century literature, though few have the tough, unsentimental edge of Baudelaire's 'The Old Mountebank': what is less usual is his depiction of the child, for while the French Romantics, like their German and English counterparts, saw childhood as a time of heightened senses, when colours, sounds, and smells are registered more intensely than in adulthood, few of Baudelaire's contemporaries added to this view the presentation of the child's sexual awareness or stressed so forcibly the links between childhood experience and adult personality.

The basic subject-matter of the prose poems is, therefore, extracted from everyday, contemporary life. In exploring these themes, Baudelaire exploits to the full both the value of lyrical hyperbole, as in 'The Desire to Paint', and the suggestive understatement of, for instance, 'The Port'. Yet if a form of

imaginative realism is a central mode in the prose poems, Baude-
laire also employs very different means, reproducing images
created by the mind when intoxicated or dreaming, drawing
on the animal fables of La Fontaine to suggest tendencies which
are unmistakably human, or forging allegorical fables to offer
explanations for the ironies of fate, or the inexplicable aspects
of individual personalities. Although it may be possible to postu-
late a formal classification of the prose poems, as David Scott[1]
(among others) does in his guide to the collection, such schema-
tizing attempts invariably simplify a complex and subtle inter-
weaving of moods and techniques. A single prose poem may
move from moments of intense lyricism to passages of sharp
analysis or deflating irony, as happens in 'The Double Bedroom'
and 'Evening Twilight', to mention just two examples.

Moreover, while for *The Flowers of Evil* Baudelaire claimed
to have employed a secret architecture, his notes indicate a
far freer structure for the volume of prose poems. We do not
know whether, had Baudelaire lived, they would have appeared
in the order chosen by his friends Asselineau and Banville for
the posthumous publication. His notes, however, use the
image of the kaleidoscope as a structuring principle, suggesting
that central themes would be explored from a variety of styles
and points of view. Certainly there are poems which seem
to present deliberate contrasts: one might think, for instance,
of the cloud-loving poet of 'The Outsider' and the practical
mistress of 'The Soup and the Clouds'; the friendly smile
exchanged between rich child and poor child in 'The Poor
Child's Toy' and the murderous battle between the two children
in 'The Cake'; the narrator's attempt to change his mistress
in 'The Wild Woman and the Little Sweetheart' and the
beloved's mocking affirmation that he must love her as she
is in 'Which is the Real Benedicta?' Nevertheless, other struc-
tural principles could be adduced on either thematic or stylistic
lines, and it is part of the work's distinctive flavour that no

---

[1] See B. Wright and D. Scott, *La Fanfarlo and Le Spleen de Paris* (London:
Grant and Cutler, 1984), chart between pp. 76 and 77.

watertight structural or thematic grid can be imposed upon it.

Stylistically, the collection is marked by Baudelaire's decision to combine certain techniques of poetry, in particular a constant underpinning of image by phonetic patterning, with the possibilities offered by prose in terms both of rapid changes of mood and of combinations of pathos and comedy, lyricism and irony. As a result, while they may not equal certain of the moments of intense beauty and extreme passion that mark *The Flowers of Evil*, the prose poems are rich in remarkable metaphors, in suggestive echoes of other literary forms, in the deliberately jarring juxtapositions that re-create the incongruity of modern life, and in a form of totally unsentimental self-mockery that would be out of place in traditional verse forms. Thus, in 'To Each His Monster', Baudelaire not only offers us the unforgettable image of a chimerical beast crushing each individual, but intensifies the visual image through the sound patterns describing the way in which the monster enveloped and oppressed each man with its powerful, elastic muscles. Moreover, while the narrator is for most of the poem a sharply observant, external witness to the scene, he too is revealed in the poem's conclusion to carry a similar burden, that laid upon him by 'unconquerable Indifference'. Similarly, in 'Which is the Real Benedicta?', Baudelaire's uncompromising but comic image of man forever caught with one leg in the grave of the ideal is given even greater intensity by the contrast between the narrative voice's precious evocation of Spring 'swinging its censer even in the cemeteries themselves' and Benedicta's vulgar depiction of herself as 'one of the real riff-raff'.

While classical mythology is one of the major sources of comparison and personification in the verse poems, the prose poems set up resonances with more banal and more recent forms of writing. Drawing on the fantastic imagery of Romanticism in ways which replace creatures of the supernatural with products of the imagination, Baudelaire depicts the writer in the following words: 'Like those wandering souls in search of a body, he enters, when he so desires, into the character of each individual'. This kind of cross-textual reference not only enriches the poem with an overlay of echo and suggestion, but also indicates an ironic and debunking shift away from Romanticism's dark concerns to a more pragmatic notion of evil as the product of man: what more urbane and yet powerful image of the devil could one imagine than that Baudelaire provides in 'The Generous Gambler', and what more cynical summing up of the pitiful heights of most human ambitions than his promise to the narrator: 'Never will you form a desire without my helping you to achieve it; you will reign over your common fellow men; you will be provided with flattery and even adoration; silver, gold, diamonds, and fairy-tale palaces will come to seek you out and beg you to accept them, without your having to make any effort to win them; you will change country as often as your fancy decrees; you will grow drunk on pleasure and never weary of it, in charming lands where the weather is always warm and where the women smell as sweet as flowers,—et cetera, et cetera ...' The language of pantomime and fairy tale also enters his prose poems, through the fairies who bestow gifts and fortune on the newly born, or the moon who lends her colours and whims to those children she singles out for special protection.

Baudelaire finds inspiration, too, in the hedonism and vulgarity of Second Empire Paris to suggest, for instance, the yawning gap between social classes in 'The Eyes of the Poor', where the decoration of the new café, for all its bad taste and conspicuous spending, seems to the impoverished bystander to have taken up all the gold that might otherwise have come to the poor. Equally, the incongruity of contemporary life is sharply, if more sympathetically, evoked in the image of the young widow, who prefers to hear a public concert from a distance, saving the money that a ticket would have cost to provide her child with something it needs or desires.

Incongruity is also something the narrator detects in himself, with a self-mockery whose astringency never relaxes into self-pity. Having happily gambled his soul away to the Devil and received the promise that all he wishes will be his, he still finds himself praying to God, beseeching him to make the Devil keep his promise. And having boldly cast aside the temptations of riches, power, and fame in dream, he finds on awakening so little honour in such a course of action that he unashamedly, but unavailingly, begs Eros, Plutus, and Glory to return when he is awake and less susceptible to scruples.

In explaining why he did not attempt a translation of Poe's poems, as he had done of his tales, Baudelaire asserted that they would lose too much were they to be stripped of the 'volupté', the physical pleasure, of rhyme and rhythm. In his prose poems, he sets aside the pleasures of regular, pre-ordained rhythm and rhyme patterns, to create metrical and phonetic patternings which correspond to the needs of his subject-matter. The opening of 'To Each His Monster' offers a fine example of this specifically prose-poetic technique, which even in translation conveys some of the force of the original: 'Under a broad grey sky, on a broad dusty plain, devoid of paths, devoid of thistles, devoid of nettles, I met several men who were walking along with bowed backs'. In the same prose poem he offers an even more intense example, where the sound patterns, moreover, recall those of his verse poem 'The Swan' and where the image is enriched by the reference to Dante's evocation of the gates of Hell with their message that all who enter must abandon hope: 'under the splenetic bowl of the sky, their feet deep in the dust of a soil as desolate as that sky, they walked with the resigned expression of those condemned to hope forever'.

Despite the undoubted mastery of the medium that such techniques reveal, and however apparently triumphal his description of the search for a literary form flexible enough to allow lyricism and analysis, vulgarity and intensity, irony and beauty, there are numerous signs that he felt towards the end of his life that he had, if not failed, at least wasted much of his energy in an experiment of insufficient importance. In a study of Poe, Baudelaire laments, in terms which seem to point to a personal conviction:

I know that in literature throughout the world efforts, often felicitous, have been made to create purely poetic tales ... but these are efforts and struggles which serve only to demonstrate the strength of the true means adapted to the corresponding aims, and I am not far from believing that in certain authors, the greatest one could choose, these heroic temptations are the fruit of despair.

Nevertheless, despite all Baudelaire's own misgivings, for the modern reader the *Short Prose Poems* is a richly rewarding, constantly challenging collection of poems which, rather than being secondary to the verse poems, is, exactly as he had wanted it to be, a fitting counterpart to them, a counterpart, moreover, which may well be closer to the temper of modern life than *The Flowers of Evil*.

NOTE ON THE TEXT

La Fanfarlo was not published in volume form during the poet's lifetime. The text used for translation is that of the Pléiade edition.

Baudelaire died before his prose poems were published. The 'definitive edition' was entrusted to his friends Charles Asselineau and Théodore de Banville, who made use of a handwritten list Baudelaire had produced giving the titles of the poems and the order in which they should appear. The text itself is based not only on manuscript versions predating publication in reviews, but also on Baudelaire's own corrections to those published in *La Presse*. This translation draws on the edition published by the Pléiade, under the editorship of Claude Pichois, on the version published by José Corti and edited by Robert Kopp, on the latter's edition for Gallimard, on that produced by Gallimard edited by D. Scott and B. Wright, and on the Manchester University Press publication, edited by M. Zimmerman.

FIRST PUBLICATIONS

La Fanfarlo, first number of *Le Bulletin de la Société des gens de lettres*, 1847; signed under the name Charles Defayis.

PROSE POEMS

'Dedication: To Arsène Houssaye', *La Presse*, 26 August 1862.

'The Outsider', *La Presse*, 26 August 1862.

'The Old Woman's Despair', *La Presse*, 26 August 1862.

'The Artist's *Confiteor*', *La Presse*, 26 August 1862.

'A Prankster', *La Presse*, 26 August 1862.

'The Double Bedroom', *La Presse*, 26 August 1862.

'To Each His Monster', *La Presse*, 26 August 1862; initial title: 'To Each his Own'.

'The Jester and the Goddess', *La Presse*, 26 August 1862.

'The Dog and the Flask', *La Presse*, 26 August 1862.

'The Bad Glazier', *La Presse*, 26 August 1862.

'One O'Clock in the Morning', *La Presse*, 27 August 1862.

'The Wild Woman and the Little Sweetheart', *La Presse*, 27 August 1862.

'The Crowds'. *Revue fantaisiste*, 1 November 1861.

'The Widows', *Revue fantaisiste*, 1 November 1861.

'The Old Mountebank', *Revue fantaisiste*, 1 November 1861.

'The Cake', *La Presse*, 24 September 1862.

'The Clock', *Le Présent*, 24 August 1857.

'A Hemisphere in a Head of Hair', *Le Présent*, 24 August 1857.

'The Invitation to a Journey', *Le Présent*, 24 August 1857.

'The Poor Child's Toy', *La Presse*, 24 September 1862.

'The Gifts of the Fairies', *La Presse*, 24 September 1862.

'The Temptations, or Eros, Plutus, and Glory', *Revue nationale et étrangère*, 10 June 1863.

'Evening Twilight', *Fontainebleau: Hommage à C. F. Denecourt* (Paris: Hachette, 1855).

'Solitude', *Fontainebleau: Hommage à C. F. Denecourt* (Paris: Hachette, 1855).

'Plans', *Le Présent*, 24 August 1857.

'Beautiful Dorothea', *Revue nationale et étrangère*, 10 June 1863.

'The Eyes of the Poor', *La Vie parisienne*, 2 July 1864, unsigned.

'A Hero's Death', *Revue nationale et étrangère*, 10 October 1863.

'The Counterfeit Coin', *L'Artiste*, 1 November 1864.

'The Generous Gambler', *Figaro*, 7 February 1864.

'The Rope', *Figaro*, 7 February 1864.

'Vocations', *Figaro*, 14 February 1864.

'The Thyrsus', *Revue nationale et étrangère*, 10 December 1863.

'Never be Sober', *Figaro*, 7 February 1864.

'Already!', *Revue nationale et étrangère*, 10 December 1863.

'The Windows', *Revue nationale et étrangère*, 10 December 1863.

SELECT BIBLIOGRAPHY

For a detailed and highly readable biography of Baudelaire see C. Pichois, *Baudelaire*, tr. G. Robb (London: Hamish Hamilton, 1989). Baudelaire's art criticism has been translated by Jonathon Mayne in two volumes: *The Mirror of Art* (London: Phaidon Press, 1955) and *The Painter of Modern Life and Other Essays* (London: Phaidon Press, 1955). M. Strong has translated his studies of intoxicants, together with writings on the same subject by Gautier: *Hashish, Wine, Opium* (London: Calder and Boyars, 1972). The range of critical works devoted to Baudelaire is, of course, enormous. What follows is a highly selective and very brief guide to good studies in English concerning the works in the present translation.

BENJAMIN, W., *Charles Baudelaire: A Lyric Poet in the Era of High Capitalism*, tr. H. Zohn (London: NLB, 1973).

ELIOT, T. S., 'Baudelaire', in *Selected Essays* (London: Faber and Faber, 1972).

HIDDLESTON, J., *Baudelaire and 'Le Spleen de Paris'* (Oxford: Oxford University Press, 1987).

MANSELL JONES, P., *Baudelaire* (Cambridge: Bowes and Bowes, 1952).

MOSSOP, D., *Baudelaire's Tragic Hero* (Oxford: Oxford University Press, 1961).

SARTRE, J. P., *Baudelaire*, tr. M. Turnell (London: Hamish Hamilton, 1964).

WING, N., 'The Poetics of Irony in Baudelaire's *La Fanfarlo*', *Neophilologus*, 59/2 (Apr. 1975), 529–71.

WRIGHT, B., and SCOTT, D., *'La Fanfarlo' and 'Le Spleen de Paris'*, Grant and Cutler Critical Guides (London: Grant and Cutler, 1984).

A CHRONOLOGY OF CHARLES BAUDELAIRE

1759 Birth at La Neuville-au-Pont of Joseph-François Baudelaire, father of C.B.

1793 Birth in London of Caroline Archenbaut Defayis, poet's mother. Her name is sometimes spelt Dufays or Dufaÿs, and C.B. occasionally uses it as a pseudonym in the 1840s. *La Fanfarlo* is signed 'Defayis'.

1819 Marriage of Joseph-François Baudelaire and Caroline Defayis.

1821 9 April: birth of Charles-Pierre Baudelaire.

1827 10 February: death of C.B.'s father.

1828 Caroline Baudelaire marries Lieutenant-Colonel Jacques Aupick.

1841 C.B. sent on a voyage, meant to take him to Calcutta. Stops at Réunion and Mauritius, then refuses to travel any further. Returns to France, arriving 15 February 1842.

1842 Inherits 100,000 francs from his father on attaining his majority.

1844 *Conseil de famille* takes control of C.B.'s fortune. Narcisse Ancelle appointed trustee.

1845 Publications of his *Salon* of 1845 and a poem, 'To a Creole Lady'.

1846 Publication of his *Salon* of 1846.

1847 Publication of *La Fanfarlo*.

1848 February Revolution and uprisings of July days find C.B. participating on the side of the revolutionaries. Collaborates on a newspaper, *Le Salut public*, of which only two numbers appeared.

1851 Publication of *Concerning Wine and Hashish*, which contains prose versions of verse poems on wine to appear in *The Flowers of Evil*. 27 September: publication of one of these poems, 'The Soul of Wine'.

1855 *La Revue des deux mondes* publishes 18 poems under the title *The Flowers of Evil*.
     June: publication of the first of C.B.'s prose poems, 'Evening Twilight' and 'Solitude'.

1857 27 April: death of General Aupick.

25 June: publication of *The Flowers of Evil*.

7 July: *The Flowers of Evil* accused of being an outrage to public decency.

20 August: C.B. condemned to pay a fine of 300 francs and suppress 6 of the poems.

24 August: publication in *Le Présent* of six prose poems.

1860   1 January: C.B. sells Poulet-Malassis and de Broise the second edition of *The Flowers of Evil*, *Artificial Paradises*, and his articles of literary and art criticism.

13 January: suffers first attack of illness.

May: publication of *Artificial Paradises*.

1861   February: second edition of *The Flowers of Evil*.

15 June–15 August: *La Revue fantaisiste* publishes nine of the ten articles that make up *Reflections on Some of My Contemporaries*.

1 November: *La Revue fantaisiste* publishes nine prose poems.

1862   26 August to 24 September: *La Presse* publishes first twenty prose poems.

1864   7 and 14 February: publication in *Figaro* of 6 prose poems, under the title *The Spleen of Paris*. This is the first appearance of this title, which is used again in the *Revue de Paris* of 25 December, which publishes a further six prose poems.

24 April: C.B. arrives in Brussels.

May–June: gives lectures and readings in Belgium. Despite professed dislike of the country and its people C.B. remains in Belgium for two years.

1866   15 March: C.B. collapses in the church of Saint-Loup at Namur.

22–3 March: C.B.'s condition worsens.

30 March: paralysis of right side.

31 March: *Le Parnasse contemporain* publishes *New Flowers of Evil*.

2 July: C.B. brought back to Paris.

1867   31 August: death of C.B.

2 September: C.B. buried at the Montparnasse cemetery.

1868   Michel Lévy begins publishing C.B.'s complete works.

1869   Publication in volume IV of the *Complete Works* of the prose poems, under the title 'Short Prose Poems'.

The Prose Poems
and La Fanfarlo

Samuel Cramer, who, in the past, signed a handful of Romantic follies under the name of Manuela de Monteverde—in the heyday of Romanticism—is the contradictory product of a wan German and a Chilean brunette. Add to this double origin a French education and a literary culture and you will be less surprised—if not satisfied and edified—by the bizarre complications of this character.—Samuel's brow is noble and pure, his eyes glitter like two drops of coffee, his nose is teasing and scoffing, his lips impudent and sensual, his chin square and despotic, his hair pretentiously Raphaelesque. He is at one and the same time immensely lazy, unlucky in his ambitions, and renowned for his unhappiness; for in his whole life he has hardly ever had ideas which are more than half-baked. The sun of laziness which incessantly glows within him vaporizes and destroys the half measure of genius that Heaven has bestowed on him. Among all those half-great men I've known in the terrible life of Paris, Samuel was, more than any other, the man of beautiful works which had been bungled; a sickly and fantastic creature whose poetry gleams far more in his person than in his works, and who, towards one o'clock in the morning, between the dazzling glow of his earth-coal fire and the ticking of a clock, has always seemed to me to be the god of impotence—a modern and hermaphrodite god—an impotence so colossal and enormous that it has become epic!

How can I make you fully acquainted with, how can I let you see clearly into, this dark nature, streaked with brilliant flashes of lightning—simultaneously lazy and enterprising—fertile in ambitious plans and laughable failures—a mind in which paradox often assumed the proportions of naïvety, and whose imagination was as vast as his solitude and laziness were absolute?—One of Samuel's most natural flaws was to consider himself the equal of those he had admired; after passionately reading a fine book, his involuntary conclusion was: 'now there's something beautiful enough to be by me!'—and from there to thinking: 'so it is by me!'—is only the space of a dash.

In today's world, this kind of character is more frequent than you think; the streets, the public promenades, the inns, and all those places that offer asylum to loungers are packed with creatures of this kind. They identify so closely with the new model that they are not far from believing that they themselves invented it.—Today you'll find them painfully deciphering the mystical pages of Plotinus* or Porphyrius;* tomorrow they'll admire how well Crébillon the younger* has expressed the flighty and French side of their character. Yesterday they chatted on familiar terms with Girolomo Cardano;* now they're playing with Sterne, or wallowing with Rabelais in all the gluttony of hyperbole. They are, moreover, so happy in each of their metamorphoses that they don't bear the slightest grudge against all those fine geniuses for preceding them in posterity's esteem.—Naïve and respectable impudence! Such a man was poor Samuel.

By birth a very honest chap, he was a bit of a knave as a hobby—an actor by temperament—he performed for himself and behind closed doors incomparable tragedies, or, to be more accurate, tragicomedies. If he felt himself touched and tickled by gaiety, he had to reveal it very clearly and our man would practise roaring with laughter. If a tear gathered at the corner of an eye at some memory, he would go to the mirror and watch himself weeping. If some girl, in an excess of brutal and puerile jealousy, scratched him with a needle or a penknife, Samuel gloried in having received a knife-wound, and when he owed a miserable 20,000 francs he would cry out joyously: 'Oh how sad and lamentable is the fate of a genius harassed for a debt of a million francs!'

Moreover, you mustn't think that he was incapable of feeling true emotions, and that passion merely touched the surface of his skin. He would have sold his shirts for a man he scarcely knew, but whom, on inspecting his brow and hand, he had established the previous day as his intimate friend. To matters of the mind and soul he brought the idle contemplation of Germanic natures—in matters of passion the swift and change-able ardour of his mother—and to the practical side of life he brought all the flaws of French vanity. He would have fought a duel for an author or artist dead these two centuries. As he had been furiously pious, he was now a passionate atheist. He was at once all the artists he had studied and all the books he had read, and yet, despite this actor's skill, he remained profoundly original. He was always the gentle, the fantastic, the lazy, the terrible, the erudite, the ignorant, the slovenly, the coquettish Samuel Cramer, the romantic Manuela de Monteverde. He would be as wild about a friend as if that friend were a woman and would love a woman as if she were a friend. He was fully conversant with the logic of all good feelings and the science of all cunning, and yet he had never succeeded in anything because he believed too firmly in the impossible.—What's astonishing in that? He was always in the process of conceiving the impossible.

There came to Samuel, one evening, the thought that he would go out; the weather was fine and the air perfumed.— Following his natural inclination for the excessive, he had equally violent and prolonged periods of seclusion and dissipation and for a long time he had remained faithfully within his lodgings. The laziness inherited from his mother, the Creole *far niente* which flowed in his veins, prevented him from suffering from the disorder of his room and the fact that his linen and his hair were excessively filthy and tangled. He combed his hair, had a wash, was able in a few minutes to rediscover the costume and the aplomb of people for whom elegance is a daily matter, then he opened the window.—A warm golden light rushed into the dusty study. Samuel marvelled at how quickly Spring had come in a few days and without warning. A warm breeze, laden with pleasant odours, made him breathe deeply—part of it rushed up to his brain and filled it with reverie and desire while the rest licentiously stirred his heart, his stomach, and his liver.—He resolutely blew out his two candles, one of which was still flickering on a volume of Swedenborg* while the other guttered on one of those shameful books which offer profitable reading only to minds obsessed with an immoderate taste for truth.

Looking down from his solitary abode, littered with packets

of paper, paved with books, and peopled with his dreams, Samuel had often noticed, walking along a path in the Luxembourg Gardens, a form and a face he had loved in the provinces——at the age when one loves love.——Her features, although they had matured and grown plumper with the passing of a few years, had the profound and decent grace of the honest woman; in the depths of her eyes there still glittered from time to time the tearful reverie of the young girl. She would walk to and fro, usually escorted by a fairly elegant maid, whose face and bearing suggested that she was more of a confidante and companion than a servant. She seemed to seek out abandoned spots and would sit sadly, with the attitude of a widow, sometimes absent-mindedly holding in her hand a book she did not read.

Samuel had known her in the neighbourhood of Lyons, when she was young, alert, playful, and slimmer. By dint of gazing at her and, as it were, recognizing her, he had rediscovered one by one all the little memories associated with her in his imagination; he had told himself, incident by incident, the whole story of their youthful romance, a story which had since been lost in the preoccupations of his life and the labyrinth of his passions.

On that evening, he greeted her, but with more care and more politeness. As he walked past her, he heard behind him this fragment of conversation:

'What do you think of that young man, Mariette?', but this was said in so absent-minded a tone that the most malicious observer would have found in it no reason to say anything against the lady.

'I think he's very fine, madam. You know that he is Samuel Cramer?'

And in a more severe tone: 'How do you know that, Mariette?'*

And that explains why on the following day Samuel was very careful to bring her her handkerchief and her book, which he found on a bench and which she had not lost, since she was close by looking at the sparrows squabbling over crumbs, or appearing to contemplate the inner workings of the vegetation. As often happens between two people whose souls a complicitous destiny has elevated to an equal pitch—engaging conversation rather abruptly—he nevertheless had the bizarre good fortune to find a person disposed to listen and reply to him.

'Could I be so fortunate, madam, as still to be lodged in a corner of your memory? Have I changed so much that you cannot recognize in me the childhood friend with whom you deigned to play hide-and-seek, and skip school?'

'A woman', the lady replied with a half smile, 'does not have the right to recognize people so easily; and that's why I thank you, sir, for taking it on yourself to offer me the chance to look back on those fine and happy memories.— And then . . . every year of our lives contains so many events and thoughts . . . and it really seems to me that many years have passed, have they not . . .?'

'Years', replied Samuel, 'which for me have sometimes passed very slowly, sometimes flown very swiftly away, but all of which have been cruel in their different ways.'

'And poetry? . . .', said the lady with a smile in her eyes.

'Still, madam!', said Samuel with a laugh. 'But what were you reading there?'

'A novel by Walter Scott.'*

'Now I understand why you interrupt your reading so often!—Oh what a boring writer!—A dusty digger-up of chronicles! a dull accumulation of descriptions of bric-à-brac!—a pile of old things and all sorts of discarded bits and pieces: armour, dishes, furniture, Gothic inns and melodramatic castles, in which wander spring-loaded dummies, clad in jerkins and brightly coloured doublets. All well-known types, that no eighteen-year-old plagiarist will still want to touch in ten years' time. Impossible chatelaines and lovers utterly lacking in any modern significance—no truth as regards the heart, no philosophy as regards the emotions! What a difference between him and our good French novelists, where passions and morals are always more important than the material description of objects!—What does it matter whether the chatelaine wears a ruff or panniers, or an Oudinot petticoat,* provided she can sob or betray fittingly? Does the lover interest you much more because he carries in his waistcoat a dagger instead of a visiting card, and does a despot in a black coat cause you a less poetic terror than a tyrant clad in buffalo skin and iron?'

Samuel, as you can see, can be classified among the *proselytizing* people—unbearable and impassioned men, whose conversation is spoilt by their profession, and for whom any occasion is worth seizing—even if it's a conversation struck up beside a tree or at the corner of a road, even with a rag-picker—to develop pig headedly their own ideas.—Between travelling salesmen, wandering industrialists, men who set up limited companies, and *proselytizing* poets there is merely the same difference as that between advertisements and sermonizing: the vice of the last-mentioned group is completely disinterested.

Well, the lady replied simply: 'My dear Mr Samuel, I am merely the public, which is as much as to say that my soul is innocent. And therefore pleasure is for me the easiest thing to find.—But let's talk of you: I would consider myself happy if you were to judge me worthy to read some of your productions.'

'But madam, how can it be that ...?' replied the enormous vanity of the astonished poet.

'The person in charge of my lending library claims he doesn't know you.'

And she gave a gentle smile to soften the effect of this fleeting dig.

'Madam', said Samuel sententiously, 'the true public of the nineteenth century is women; your support will establish me more firmly than would that of twenty academies.'

'Well, sir, I'll count on your promise.—Mariette, my sunshade and my scarf; at home *they* may be impatient for us to return. You know that my husband comes home early.'

She gave him a graciously shortened bow, which was in no way compromising and in which familiarity did not exclude dignity.

Samuel was not surprised to find an old provincial love now tied to the conjugal yoke. In the universal history of sentiment, that is indispensable.

Her name was Mme de Cosmelly, and she lived in one of the most aristocratic streets of the faubourg Saint-Germain.

The following day he found her, her head bowed by a gracious and almost studied melancholy towards the flowers in the bed, and he offered her a volume of *Ospreys*, a collection of sonnets, of the kind we have all written and all read in the days when our judgement was so short and our hair so long.*

Samuel was very curious to know if his *Ospreys* had charmed the soul of that melancholy beauty and if the cries of those evil birds had spoken to her in his favour; but a few days later she said to him with maddening candour and honesty: 'Sir, I am only a woman, and as a result my judgement is worth little; but it seems to me that the sorrows and loves of authors bear hardly any resemblance to the sorrows and loves of other men. You address what are doubtless very elegant, exquisitely chosen chivalrous remarks to ladies whom I esteem highly enough to believe that they must occasionally be shocked by them. You sing of the beauty of mothers in a style which must deprive you of the support of their daughters. You tell the world that you are mad about the foot and the hand of Mrs So-and-so who, let us suppose it for the sake of her honour, spends less time in reading you than in knitting stockings and mittens for the feet and hands of her children. By one of the most extraordinary contrasts, the mysterious cause of which still escapes me, you reserve your most mystical incense for bizarre creatures who read even less often than the ladies and you swoon platonically before the sultanas of lowly places, who, when they see the delicate person of a poet, must, I imagine, open their eyes as wide as animals awakened by a fire. Moreover, I cannot imagine why you cherish such deeply morbid subjects and anatomical descriptions. When you're young and you have, as you do, a fine talent and all the conditions considered necessary for happiness, it seems to me far more natural to celebrate the health and the joys of the honest man than to train yourself to curse, and to discourse with *Ospreys*.'

This is what he replied: 'Madam, pity me, or rather pity us, for I have many brothers like me: it is our hatred of everyone

including ourselves that has led us to these lies. It's despair
at being unable to be handsome and noble by natural means
that has led us to make up our faces so bizarrely. We have
applied ourselves so intensely to corrupting our hearts, we have
so abused the microscope to study the hideous excrescences
and the shameful warts with which our hearts are covered and
which we take pleasure in enlarging, that it is impossible for
us to talk in the same tongue as other men. They live to live
and we, alas!, live to know. Therein lies all the mystery. The
passing years change only our voices, all they destroy is our
hair and our teeth; it is we ourselves who have changed the
accents of nature, we have plucked out one by one the virginal
modesties which bristled within us when we were honest men.
We have psychologized like madmen, who increase their mad-
ness by trying to understand it. The years weaken only our
limbs; it is we who have deformed our passions. Accursed, thrice
accursed be our infirm fathers who brought us rickety and un-
timely into the world, predestined as we are to give birth only
to still-born children!'

'Yet more *Ospreys*!' she said. 'Listen, just give me your arm
and let's admire these poor flowers that Spring has made so
happy!'

Instead of admiring the flowers, Samuel Cramer, inspired
with periods and sentences, began to translate into prose and
declaim a handful of bad stanzas which he had composed in
his first manner. The lady let him do so.

'How things change, how little of the same man there
remains, apart from memory! But memory is merely a fresh
source of suffering. What wonderful days they were when morn-
ing never awakened us with our knees stiff or aching from the
weariness of dreams, when our bright eyes laughed at all of
nature, when our soul did not reason, but lived and enjoyed;
when our sighs flowed gently and silently, with no trace of
pride! How often, in the leisure of imagination, have I seen
again one of those beautiful autumnal evenings when young
souls make as much progress as those trees which grow several
feet after being struck by lightning! Then I see, I feel, I under-
stand; the moon awakens the plump moths; the warm breeze

opens the evening flowers; the water in the great fountains sleeps. Imagine you can hear the sudden waltzes played on that mysterious piano. The perfumes of the storm come in through the windows; it is the hour when the gardens are full of pink and white dresses which are not afraid of getting damp. The accommodating bushes catch flying skirts; brown hair and blond curls whirl around together!—Do you still remember, madam, the enormous haystacks which we slipped down so quickly, the old nurse who pursued us so slowly, and the bell which so promptly called you back under the eye of your aunt in the great dining room?'

Mme de Cosmelly interrupted Samuel with a sigh, tried to open her mouth, no doubt to beg him to stop, but he had already started talking again.

'What is most distressing,' he said, 'is the fact that all love affairs always end badly, and the more divine and ethereal their beginnings, the worse their end. There is no dream, however ideal, which one doesn't rediscover with a greedy nurseling clinging to her breast; there is no hiding place, no little house so delicious and so abandoned that the mattock doesn't come to destroy it. At least such destruction is merely material; but there is a more pitiless and secret form of destruction which attacks the invisible. Imagine that at the moment when you whisper in the ear of your chosen companion: "Let's fly together to the furthermost reaches of the heavens!"—an implacable and serious voice in your ear tells you that our passions are liars, that it is our short-sightedness that creates beautiful faces, and our ignorance that makes beautiful souls, and that there must necessarily come a day when the idol, to more clear-sighted eyes is nothing more that an object not of hatred, but of scorn and astonishment!'

'Have pity, sir!', said Mme de Cosmelly. She was obviously moved; Samuel could see that he had driven his sword into an old wound and he insisted with cruelty.

'Madam', he said, 'the salutary sufferings of memory have their own charm, and in this intoxication of unhappiness one can sometimes find relief.—At that funereal warning, all loyal souls cry out: "Lord, take me from here together with my dream, intact and pure; I want to give back to nature my passion with all its virginity and bear elsewhere my unwithered crown." Moreover, the results of disillusionment are terrible.—The sickly children of a dying love are sad debauchery and hideous impotence: the debauchery of the mind, the impotence of the heart, which means that the first lives only through curiosity and the second dies each day of weariness. We are all more or less like a voyager who has travelled over a very vast country and each evening watches the sun, which but recently cast its superb golden glow on the attractions of the route, sink to rest below a flat horizon. He sits down resignedly on one of the dirty hills covered with unknown debris and tells the perfumes of the heather that they drift upwards in vain to the empty sky: he tells the scarce and ill-starred seeds that it is in vain that they germinate in the baked earth; the birds who believe their unions blessed by someone that they are wrong to build nests in a land swept by cold, rough winds. Sadly he resumes his journey towards a desert which he knows to be like the one he has just crossed, escorted by a pale ghost he calls Reason, who lights with a pale lantern the aridity of his path and who, to quench the growing thirst for passion which grips him from time to time, pours him the poison of boredom.'

Suddenly, hearing a deep sigh and a poorly suppressed sob, he turned to Mme de Cosmelly; she was weeping copiously and did not even have the strength to hide her tears.

He gazed at her for a while in silence, with the most tender and unctuous air that he could assume; the brutal and hypocritical actor was proud of those fine tears; he considered them as his work and his literary property. He was mistaken about the intimate meaning of that grief, as Mme de Cosmelly, drowning in that candid despair, was mistaken about the meaning of his gaze. There took place a singular play of misinterpretations, at the end of which Samuel Cramer definitively held out both hands to her and she accepted them with tender trust.

'Madam', Samuel remarked after a few instants of silence—the classical silence of emotion—'true wisdom consists less in cursing than in hoping. Without that utterly divine gift of hope, how could we cross that hideous desert of boredom I've just

described to you? The ghost that accompanies us is truly a
ghost of reason: one can drive it away by sprinkling it with
holy water of the first theological strength. There is an amiable
philosophy that is able to find consolation in what appear to
be the most unworthy objects. In the same way that virtue
is better than innocence, and that there is more merit in planting
seeds in the desert than in carelessly gathering fruit in a fertile
orchard, so is it truly worthy of a higher nature to purify itself
and to purify its neighbours by its contact. As there is no betrayal
which cannot be pardoned, there is no fault for which one
cannot gain absolution, no lapse of memory which cannot be
restored; there is an art to loving one's neighbour and finding
him lovable, as there is an art to knowing how to live well.
The more delicate a spirit, the more original beauties it dis-
covers; the more tender a soul, and the more open to divine
hope, the more it finds in others, however sullied they may
be, reasons for loving them; this is a work of charity, and more
than one voyager, desolate and lost in the arid deserts of dis-
illusionment, has been seen to reconquer faith and fall all the
more deeply in love with what she had lost, with all the more
reason in that she then possesses the knowledge of how to direct
her passion and that of the person she loves.'

Mme de Cosmelly's face had slowly cleared; her sadness
gleamed with hope like a damp sun and scarcely had Samuel
finished his speech than she said to him intensely with the naïve
ardour of a child:

'Is it really true, sir, that such a thing is possible? Are there
for those who are in despair branches which are as easy as
that to seize?'

'There certainly are, madam.'

'Oh! you would truly make me the happiest of women if
you would deign to teach me your recipes.'

'It's the easiest thing in the world', he answered brutally.

In the course of this sentimental banter, trust had come and
united the hands of the couple; with the result that after a
few hesitations and pruderies which seemed to Samuel to bode
well, Mme de Cosmelly in her turn confided in him, beginning
with the following words:

'I understand all that a poetic soul can suffer in such isolation and how quickly an ambition held by a heart such as yours must waste away in loneliness; but your sufferings, which belong to you alone, come, as far as I could make out amidst the pomp and ceremony of your words, from bizarre needs which are always unsatisfied and all but impossible to satisfy. You suffer, it's true; but it may well be that your suffering will create your greatness and that it is as necessary to you as happiness is to others.—Now, will you deign to listen to, and sympathize with, sorrows which are easier to understand—a provincial sorrow? I expect from you, M. Cramer, from you as a learned and intellectual man, the advice and perhaps the help of a friend.

'In the days when you knew me I was a good little girl, already slightly dreamy, as you yourself were, but shy and very obedient; you know that I looked at myself in the mirror less often than you did and that I always hesitated to eat or put in my pockets the peaches and grapes that you would boldly go and steal for me in our neighbour's orchard. I never found pleasure truly agreeable and complete except in so far as it was permitted, and I much preferred to kiss a handsome lad like you in front of my aunt than in the fields. The coquetry and the care that any young girl in search of a husband must put into her appearance came to me only late. When I knew more or less how to sing a romance at the piano, I was dressed with more attention and I was forced to stand up straight; I had to do exercises, and I was forbidden to spoil my hands by planting flowers or bringing up birds. I was allowed to read other books apart from Berquin* and was taken in full evening dress to the local theatre to see bad operas. When M. de Cosmelly came to the manor house I first felt a lively friendship for him, comparing his flourishing youth with the somewhat scolding old age of my aunt, I found him moreover noble and honest and he treated me with the most respectful chivalry. And, too, they told me the most attractive stories about him: an arm broken in a duel for a rather cowardly friend who had entrusted to him his sister's honour, enormous sums lent to former schoolmates who had no money of their own; and so forth. He adopted towards everyone an air of command

which was at once affable and irresistible and which conquered
me as well. What sort of life he had led before coming to the
manor house; whether he had known other pleasures apart
from hunting with me or singing virtuous romances accom-
panied by my poor piano; whether he had had mistresses; I
had no idea and it did not occur to me to try to find out.
I fell in love with him with all the credulity of a young girl
who has had no time to make comparisons and I married him—
which gave my aunt the greatest pleasure. When I was his
wife in the eyes of the Church and the law, I loved him even
more.—I loved him far too much, no doubt.—Was I right or
wrong? Who can know? I was happy in that love and I was
wrong to be unaware that it could be disturbed.—Did I know
him well before marrying him? No, I probably didn't. But it
seems one can no more accuse an honest girl who wants to
marry of making an unwise choice than one can accuse a fallen
woman for taking an ignoble lover. Both women—how unfortu-
nate we are!—are equally ignorant. What they lack, these
unhappy victims known as girls in search of a husband, is an
education in shame, and by that I mean the knowledge of male
vices. I would like each of these poor little things, before submit-
ting to the conjugal yoke, to be able to hear, in a secret place,
from which they could not be seen, two men chatting together
about life and above all about women. After that first and
redoubtable test, they could then hand themselves over with
less danger to the terrible chances of marriage, knowing the
strengths and weaknesses of their future tyrants.'

Samuel did not know exactly where this charming victim
was heading; but he was beginning to feel that, for a disillusioned
wife, she spoke far too much about her husband.

After a pause of a few minutes, as if fearing to approach
the baleful spot, she continued in the following words: 'One
day, M. de Cosmelly wanted to return to Paris; it was essential
that I should shine in my true light and that I be seen in a
setting worthy of my merits. A beautiful and educated woman,
he used to say, ought to be in Paris. She has to know how
to pose before society and allow a few of her rays to fall on
her husband.—A wife whose mind has nobility and common

sense knows she can have no glory in this world except in so far as she derives glory from him in whose company she travels; she knows that she adds to his virtues and above all that she is respected only in so far as she makes him respected.— No doubt this was the simplest and surest way of making himself obeyed almost joyously; I certainly did not need the knowledge that my efforts and my obedience would embellish me in his eyes to make me decide to approach that terrible Paris of which I was instinctively afraid and whose black and dazzling phantom standing on the horizon of my dreams crushed my poor little loving heart.—Therein, according to what he said, lay the true motive of the voyage. A husband's vanity creates virtue in a loving wife. Perhaps he lied even to himself with a degree of good faith and cheated his conscience without really realizing it.—In Paris we had days reserved for close friends with whom M. de Cosmelly at length grew bored just as he had grown bored with his wife. Perhaps he was a little weary of her, because she loved him too much; she wore her entire heart on her sleeve. He became disgusted with his friends for the opposite reason. All they had to offer him was the monotonous pleasure of conversations in which passion has no part to play. Henceforth his activity took another direction. After friends came horses and gambling. The hubbub of the world, the sight of those who had remained unshackled and who ceaselessly recounted memories of a mad and busy youth dragged him from the fireside and from long chats. He, who had never had any occupations other than his heart, had affairs. Since he was rich and without a profession he was able to create for himself numerous restless and frivolous occupations which filled his entire time; conjugal questions such as 'Where are you going?', 'When can we expect you home? Come back soon.'—had to be thrust to the bottom of my heart; for the English life-style, that death of the heart, the life of clubs and circles, absorbed him utterly.—The exclusive care he took of his person and the way he affected the airs of a dandy were what shocked me first; it was obvious that they were not directed at me. I wanted to do as he did, to be more beautiful, that is more seductive, seductive for him, as he was for the world; in the past I had offered everything, given everything, henceforth I wanted to make him beg me for it. I wanted to reawaken the cinders of my extinguished happiness by shaking and turning them; but where ruse is concerned I must be clumsy, and as regards vice I must be awkward, for he didn't deign to notice.— My aunt, cruel as are all old and envious women, who are reduced to admiring a spectacle in which they themselves used once to be actresses, and forced to contemplate the pleasures that are refused to them, was very careful to inform me, through the self-interested intervention of one of M. de Cosmelly's cousins, that he had fallen in love with a very popular theatre girl. I arranged to have myself escorted to all the plays and every time a slightly pretty woman stepped on to the stage I trembled at the thought that in her I might be admiring my rival. At last I learnt, through the charity of the same cousin, that it was La Fanfarlo, a dancer as stupid as she is beautiful.— You who are an author, you surely know her.—I am not very vain, nor am I very proud of my face; but I can swear to you, M. Cramer, that many a night towards three or four in the morning, weary from waiting for my husband, my eyes red with tears and insomnia, after having pleaded in lengthy prayers for his return to fidelity and duty, I asked God, my conscience, and my mirror, if I were as lovely as that miserable Fanfarlo. My mirror and my conscience replied: yes. God forbade me to glory in it but not to draw from it a legitimate victory. Why is it, then, that between two equal beauties, men often prefer the flower whose perfume all and sundry have breathed in, to the one that has always kept herself away from passers-by in the best-hidden paths of the conjugal garden? Why should it be that women who are prodigal with their bodies, those treasures to which one sultan alone should have the key, possess more admirers than the rest of us, we unfortunate martyrs who love but once? What is the singularly magic charm with which vice casts its halo around certain creatures? What clumsy and repulsive aspect does virtue bestow on those who are virtuous? Answer me, you who, because of your profession, must know all the sentiments of life and their diverse causes!'

Samuel had no time to reply, for she went on heatedly: 'M.

de Cosmelly has very serious concerns on his conscience, if the loss of a pure, young soul is of interest to the God who created it to give happiness to another. If M. de Cosmelly were to die this very evening, he would have many pardons to crave; for, through his fault, he taught his wife to feel horrible emotions, hatred, and distrust of the beloved, the thirst for revenge.——Oh, sir! I spend most painful nights, deeply disturbed periods of insomnia; I pray, I curse, I blaspheme. The priest told me that one must bear one's cross with resignation; but maddened love and shaken faith do not know resignation. My confessor is not a woman, and I love my husband, I love him with all the passion and all the grief of a mistress who has been beaten and trampled under foot. There is nothing I have not tried. Instead of the dark and simple clothes which pleased his eyes in the past, I have worn mad, sumptuous outfits like those worn by actresses. I, the chaste spouse he sought out in the depths of a poor manor house, I have paraded before him in dresses worthy of a prostitute; I forced myself to be witty and playful when death was in my heart, I spangled my despair with glittering smiles. Alas! He noticed nothing. I wore rouge, sir, I even wore rouge!——You can see that it's a banal story, the story of all unfortunate women—a provincial novel!'

While she was sobbing, Samuel assumed the air of Tartuffe* seized by Orgon, the unexpected husband who leaps out of his hiding place just as the virtuous sobs of the lady leapt from her heart and seized our poet's staggering hypocrisy by the scruff of the neck.

Mme de Cosmelly's utter abandonment of constraint, the freedom and trust with which she acted had prodigiously emboldened him—without surprising him. Samuel Cramer, who often astonished the world, was rarely astonished himself. He seemed to want to put Diderot's* maxim into practice in his own life and reveal its truth: 'Incredulity is sometimes the vice of a fool, and credulity the flaw of an intelligent man. The intelligent man sees far into the immensity of what is possible. The fool sees hardly anything as possible apart from what is. This may perhaps be what makes the one pusillanimous and the other rash.' This provides an answer to everything. Some scrupulous readers, lovers of realistic truth, will no doubt find much to criticize in this tale, in which, however, I've had nothing to do, apart from changing the names and highlighting details; how, they will say, could Samuel, a poet of bad tone and poor morals, approach with such ease a woman like Mme de Cosmelly? how could he pour out to her, apropos a novel of Scott, a torrent of banal romantic poetry? And how could Mme de Cosmelly, the discreet and virtuous spouse, pour out so promptly to him, with neither modesty nor distrust, the secret of her sorrows? To which I reply that Mme de Cosmelly was as simple as a beautiful soul and that Samuel was as bold as butterflies, cockchafers, and poets; he would throw himself into every flame and come in through every window. Diderot's maxim explains why the one was so free of constraints and the other so abrupt and impudent. It also explains all the errors Samuel committed in the course of his life, errors a fool would not have committed. That section of the public which is essentially pusillanimous will hardly understand the character of Samuel, who was essentially credulous and imaginative, to such an extent that he believed—as a poet, in his public; as a man, in his own passions.

From that point he realised that this woman had more strength and depth than at first appeared, and that her candid piety should not be directly affronted. He span his romantic jargon for her again. Ashamed at having been stupid, he tried to play the roué; he also spoke to her for some time in the dialect adopted in the seminary about wounds to be closed or cauterized by the opening of new wounds which would bleed abundantly and without causing pain. If, without possessing the absolute power of a Valmont* or a Lovelace,* you have ever tried to win an honest woman who has almost no desire to be won, then you know with what laughable and emphatic clumsiness everyone says in revealing his heart: 'take my white elephant'—so this will dispense me from the need to explain to you how stupid Samuel was.—Mme de Cosmelly, that amiable Elmire* who possessed the clear and prudent gaze of virtue, immediately saw how she could use this tyro scoundrel, for her own happiness and for her husband's honour. She repaid him, therefore, in the same coin; she let him squeeze her hands;

they spoke of friendship and platonic matters. She murmured the word 'vengeance'; she said that in those painful crises that a woman goes through in the course of her life, she is willing to give to her avenger what remains of the heart that the perfidious one has been kind enough to leave—and other idle banter and dramatic silliness. In a word, she employed seduction for the right reason, and our young roué, who was more of a nitwit than a sage, promised to wrest La Fanfarlo from M. de Cosmelly and to free him of the courtesan—hoping to find in the arms of the honest woman a reward for this meritorious deed.—Only poets can be candid enough to invent such monstrosities.

A fairly comic detail in this story, which provided a kind of interlude in the painful drama which was to be played out between these four people, was the quid pro quo over Samuel's sonnets; for, where sonnets were concerned he was incorrigible—one for Mme de Cosmelly, in which he praised in mystic tones her beauty worthy of Beatrix, her voice, the angelic purity of her eyes, the chastity of her gait, etc., and the other for La Fanfarlo, in which he served up a stew of gallant remarks so highly spiced as to bring the blood to the most experienced palate, a type of poetry, moreover, in which he excelled and in which he had from an early stage gone beyond all possible Andalouseries.* The first piece went to the actress who threw this plate of cucumbers in her cigar box; the second went to the poor grass widow, who at first opened her eyes very wide, finally understood, and could not help bursting into laughter as in the good old days.

Samuel went to the theatre and set about studying La Fanfarlo on the boards. He found her light, magnificent, energetic, full of good taste in her outfits, and he judged M. de Cosmelly very fortunate to be able to ruin himself for such a morsel.

He visited her home twice—a small house with a velvet-covered staircase, full of curtains and rugs, in a new and verdant quarter of the city; but he could find no reasonable pretext for entering. A declaration of love would have been utterly useless and even dangerous. A failure would have made it impossible to return. As for getting someone to introduce him,

he learnt that La Fanfarlo received no one. A few intimate
friends saw her from time to time. What could he have to
say or do in the house of a dancer who was highly paid, magnifi-
cently maintained, and whose lover adored her? What could
he bring to her, he who was neither a tailor nor a dressmaker
nor a ballet master nor a millionaire?—He therefore came to
a simple and brutal decision: La Fanfarlo would have to come
to him. In those days, articles of praise or criticism carried
much more weight than they do now. *The successes* of the review
column, as a good lawyer said recently in a sadly famous trial,
were much greater than they are today; a few talented people
having occasionally capitulated to the journalists, the insolence
of the giddy and adventurous young knew no bounds. Samuel
therefore undertook— he who knew not a word of music—to
specialise in the lyric theatres.

From that moment on La Fanfarlo was slated every week
in the review column of an important paper. One could not
say or even imply that her legs, her ankles, or her knees were
ill shaped; her muscles rippled under her stocking and all the
lorgnettes would have cried that such an accusation was blas-
phemy. She was accused of being brutal, common, bereft of
any taste, of wanting to import into the theatre habits from
beyond the Rhine and the Pyrenees, castanets, spurs, heeled
boots—not to mention that she drank like a trooper, that she
was too fond of little dogs and her gate-keeper's daughter—and
other scraps of dirty washing from her private life, things on
which certain little papers feed and feast. She was contrasted,
using those tactics typical of journalists, which consist in compar-
ing two things which have nothing in common, with an airy
ballet dancer, who was always dressed in white and whose chaste
movements left all consciences in repose. Sometimes La Fan-
farlo would shout out and laugh very loudly towards the stalls
as she completed a leap above the footlights; she dared to dance
even when she walked. She never wore those insipid gauze
dresses which show everything and leave nothing to the imagina-
tion. She loved materials which are noisy, long skirts which
crackle and sparkle, dresses covered with tin plate which have
to be lifted very high by a vigorous knee, mountebank's bodices;

she danced not with rings, but with pendants, in her ears—I'd almost dare to call them chandeliers. She would have willingly attached to the hems of her skirts a crowd of bizarre little dolls, like the old gypsy women who tell your fortune in threatening tones and whom you meet at high noon under the arches of Roman ruins; and all this drollery moreover aroused in the romantic Samuel, one of the last romantics France possesses, extreme delight.

With the result that, after having denigrated La Fanfarlo for three months, he fell madly in love with her and she at last wanted to know what kind of monster, what heart of bronze, what philistine, what poor mind could deny so pig headedly the royalty of her genius.

You have to pay this justice to La Fanfarlo, that all she felt was a movement of curiosity, nothing more. Could such a man really have his nose in the middle of his face and was he formed entirely the same as all his fellow men? Once she had discovered one or two things about Samuel Cramer, and had learnt he was a man like any other, with a degree of sense and some talent, she realised vaguely that there was something odd in all this, and that the terrible Monday article was very likely nothing more nor less than a special kind of weekly bouquet or the visiting card of a stubborn wooer.

He found her one evening in her dressing room. Two vast torches and a large fire shed their trembling reflections on the brightly coloured costumes which were scattered around this boudoir.

The queen of the place, on the point of leaving the theatre, was resuming the garb of the simple mortal, and, bending over from her chair, was, without any false modesty, lacing her shoes to her admirable legs. Her hands, which were plump but tapering, sent her shoe-lace playing through the eyes as if it were an agile shuttle, heedless of the fact that she had to fling back her skirts. That leg was already, for Samuel, the object of eternal desire. Long, slim, strong, plump and sinewy all at the same time, it had all the correctness of the beautiful and all the licentious attraction of the pretty. Sliced perpendicularly where it was broadest, this leg would have given a

kind of triangle whose summit would have been situated on
the tibia and whose convex base would have been provided
by the rounded line of the calf. A true man's leg is too hard,
the women's legs pencilled by Devéria* are too soft to give
an idea.

In that agreeable attitude, her head, leaning towards her
foot, revealed a proconsul's neck, broad and strong, and allowed
one to imagine her shoulder-blades, covered with abundant
brown flesh. Her heavy, tightly bound hair fell forward on either
side of her neck, tickling her bosom and getting in her eyes
so that at every instant she had to brush it aside and throw
it backwards. A mischievous and charming impatience like that
of a spoilt child who considers that things aren't moving quickly
enough, ran through the entire woman and all her clothes,
and revealed at every moment new viewpoints, new effects of
line and colour.

Samuel stopped respectfully—or pretended to stop respect-
fully; for with that devil of a man, the great problem is always
to know where the actor begins.

'Ah, there you are, sir!' she said to him, without interrupting
what she was doing, although she had been warned a few
minutes before that Samuel was coming.—'You've got some-
thing to ask of me, haven't you?'

The sublime impudence of this statement went straight to
poor Samuel's heart: he would have chattered like a romantic
magpie for a week with Mme de Cosmelly; here, he replied
tranquilly: 'Yes, madam.' And his eyes filled with tears.

This had an enormous success; La Fanfarlo smiled.

'Whatever has been eating you, to set upon me so viciously?
What a horrible profession ...'

'Horrible indeed, madam. The thing is that I adore you.'

'So I suspected,' replied La Fanfarlo. 'But you're a monster;
your tactics were abominable.—To do such a thing to us poor
girls,' she added, laughing. 'Flora, my bracelet.—Give me your
arm as far as my carriage and tell me if you thought I was
on form this evening?'

So off they went, arm in arm, like two old friends; Samuel
was in love or at least he felt his heart pounding.—He was per-

haps bizarre, but certainly on that occasion he was not ridiculous.

In his joy he had almost forgotten to send word to Mme de Cosmelly about his success and to bring some hope into her deserted hearth.

A few days later. La Fanfarlo was performing the role of Columbine in a vast pantomime written for her by men of wit. In it, she appeared through an agreeable series of metamorphoses in the roles of Columbine, Marguerite, Elvire, and Zéphyrine,* and received, in utter gaiety, the kisses of several generations of men borrowed from various countries and various literatures. A great musician had not disdained to write a fantastic score, befitting the bizarre nature of the subject. La Fanfarlo was by turns decent, fairy-like, mad, frolicsome; she was sublime in her art, as much of an actress with her legs as a dancer with her eyes.

In France we have too low an opinion of the art of dance, be it said in parentheses. All the great races, starting with those of antiquity, those of India and Arabia, have cultivated it to the same extent as poetry. Dance is as far above music, at least for certain pagan organizations, as the visible and the created are above the invisible and the uncreated. Only those minds will understand me in whom music inspires ideas connected with painting. Dance can reveal all the mystery that music hides. and it has the further merit of being human and palpable. Dance is poetry with arms and legs, it's matter, gracious and terrible. animated and embellished by movement. Terpsichore is a Muse of the South; I presume she was very brown and that she often moved her feet in the golden corn; each of her movements, full of a precise cadence, provides the sculptor with a divine motif. But La Fanfarlo was a Catholic and, not content merely to compete with Terpsichore, called to her aid all the art of more modern divinities. The mists mingle shapes of fairies and water-nymphs who are less vaporous and less nonchalant. She was simultaneously a caprice by Shakespeare and a piece of Italian clowning.

The poet was delighted. He believed that he had before his eyes the dreams of his earliest days. He would willingly have jumped around in the theatre in a ridiculous way, and would have battered his head against something in the mad intoxication that dominated him.

A low and well-closed barouche whisked the poet and the dancer off to the little house I've described.

Our man expressed his admiration in silent kisses which he fervently applied to her feet and hands.—She too greatly admired him, not that she was unaware of the powers exerted by her charms, but she had never seen so bizarre a man nor so electric a passion.

The weather was as black as the grave, and the wind which rocked the heaped-up clouds crashed them together and brought a shower of hail and rain pouring down. A great storm set the attics trembling and the steeples groaning; the gutter, that funereal bed down which flow the previous day's love letters and orgies, swept its thousands of secrets bubbling down to the sewers; mortality swooped joyously down on the hospitals, and the Chattertons and Savages* of the rue Saint-Jacques grasped their desks with frozen fingers—when the most false, most selfish, most sensual, most greedy, and most witty of our friends appeared before a fine supper and an excellent table, in the company of one of the most beautiful women nature has formed to delight the eyes. Samuel wanted to open the window to gaze victoriously down on the accursed city; then lowering his eyes to the various joys he had beside him, he hurried to enjoy them.

In the company of such things, he had to be eloquent: so although his brow was too high, although his hair stuck up like a virgin forest, and although his was the nose of a snuff-taker, La Fanfarlo found him almost attractive.

Samuel and La Fanfarlo had exactly the same ideas on cooking and on the sort of food needed by creatures of the élite. Insipid meats, pallid fish were excluded from that siren's suppers. Champagne rarely dishonoured her table. The most famous Bordeaux, those with the finest bouquets, made way for the heavy, close-packed battalion of Burgundies, of wines from the Auvergne, from Anjou and the south, and foreign wines, German, Greek, Spanish. Samuel was wont to say that a glass of real wine should resemble a bunch of black grapes and contain more to eat than to drink.—La Fanfarlo loved meats which dripped blood and wines which bring intoxication. Moreover, she never got tipsy.—Both professed a sincere and profound esteem for the truffle.—The truffle, Cybele's silent and mysterious growth, that tasty illness she hides in her entrails longer than the most precious metal, that exquisite substance which defies the agronomist's science, as gold defies the science of Paracelsus,* the truffle which traces the frontier between the ancient world and the modern world,[1] and which, taken before a glass of Scio, has the same effect as several zeros after a number.

As for the question of sauces, relishes, and seasonings, a grave matter which would demand a chapter as grave as a scientific treatise, I can confirm that they were in perfect agreement, above all on the need to call all of nature's pharmacy to the aid of cooking. Spices, English powders, saffrons, colonial substances, exotic dusts, everything struck them as good, even including musk and incense. Had Cleopatra still been alive, I consider it certain that she would have sought to accompany filets of steak or venison with Arabian perfumes. Of course, it is deplorable that today's leading cooks are not obliged by a special, voluptuary law to know the chemical properties of substances, and that they do not know how to discover, when necessary, as, for example, when there is a lovers' feast, culinary elements which, like prussic acid, are almost flammable, and run swiftly through the entire organic system, and those which turn to gas as ether does.

Curiously enough, the extent to which they were in agreement over what makes for good living, and the similarity of their tastes, bound them strongly together; the deep understanding of sensual life, that gleamed in Samuel's every glance and word, greatly struck La Fanfarlo. His way of talking which was sometimes as brutal as a number, sometimes as delicate and scented as a flower or a sachet, that strange conversation, of which he alone had the secret, completed his conquest of this charming woman's good graces. Neither was it, moreover, with-

The truffles of the Romans were white and of another species. CB

out a deep and lively satisfaction that he recognized, on inspect-
ing the bedroom, a perfect fraternity of tastes and sentiments
as regards internal furnishing and construction. Cramer had
a deep hatred, and in this I believe he was perfectly justified,
of long straight lines in apartments, and of architecture imported
into domestic interiors. The vast rooms of old manor houses
fill me with fear, and I pity the chatelaines for having been
obliged to make love in those great dormitories which look
like graveyards, in vast catafalques which are called beds, on
enormous monuments which take on the pseudonym of arm-
chairs. The apartments in Pompeii are the size of your hand;
the Indian ruins which cover the Malabar coast bear witness
to the same system. These great, voluptuous, knowledgeable
peoples have a perfect understanding of the question. Intimate
emotions can be garnered only at leisure and in a very narrow
space.

La Fanfarlo's bedroom was, therefore, very small and low,
cluttered with objects which were soft, perfumed, and dangerous
to touch; the air, laden with bizarre fumes, made you long
to die slowly there as in a hot house. The lamplight played
on a jumble of lace and materials of a violent but ambiguous
colour. Here and there, on the wall, it lit paintings rich in
Spanish sensuality: very white flesh against very dark back-
grounds. It was in the depths of this ravishing slum, which
offered a cross between a den of iniquity and a sanctuary, that
Samuel saw walking towards him the new goddess of his heart,
in the radiant and sacred splendour of her nudity.

Who is the man who would not wish, even if it cost him
half his life, to see his dream, his true dream posing before
him without a single veil, and the adored phantom of his imagi-
nation dropping one by one all the garments invented to protect
her from the eyes of the profane? But would you believe that
Samuel, seized by a bizarre whim, began to shout like a spoilt
child: 'I want Columbine, give Columbine back to me; give
her back to me just as she appeared to me on the evening
when she drove me mad with her fantastic outfit and her
mountebank's bodice!'

La Fanfarlo, although at first astonished, was quite willing to humour the eccentricity of the man she had chosen, and Flora was summoned. It was in vain that she protested that it was three in the morning, that everything was shut at the theatre, the porter would be asleep, the weather was atrocious—the storm continued its uproar—she had to obey the woman who was herself obeying, and the maid left; when Cramer, struck by a new idea, dragged on the bell-pull and shouted with a thundering voice: 'Hey! don't forget the rouge.'

This characteristic detail, which was recounted by La Fanfarlo herself, one evening when her friends were asking her about the beginnings of her liaison with Samuel, did not astonish me in the slightest; I could perfectly well recognize in it the author of the *Ospreys*. He will always love rouge and greasepaint, fake gold and gewgaws of all sorts. He would happily repaint the trees and the sky, and if God had entrusted the plan of Nature to him, he would probably have spoilt it.

Although Samuel's imagination was depraved, or perhaps because it was depraved, love, in his case, was less a matter of the senses than of the mind. It was above all an admiration and an appetite for beauty; he considered reproduction as a vice of love, pregnancy as a spider's illness. Somewhere or other he has written: 'Angels are hermaphrodites and sterile.'—He loved the human body as a material harmony, as a fine piece of architecture possessing the power of movement: and that absolute materialism was not far removed from the purest idealism. But since he maintained that in beauty, which is the cause of love, there are two elements: line and attraction—and since all this concerns only the line—the attraction for him, at least on that evening, was the rouge.

La Fanfarlo brought together for him, therefore, the line and the attraction; and when she was seated on the edge of the bed in the carefree and victorious calm of the loved woman, her hands delicately placed upon him, he looked at her and he thought he saw infinity behind the light eyes of that beauty, and eventually he felt that his own eyes floated in immense horizons. Moreover, as happens to exceptional men, he was often alone in his paradise, for no one could inhabit it with him; and if, by chance, he seized her and dragged her there almost by force, she always remained behind him: and so it was that in the heaven in which he reigned, love began to grow sad and ill from this melancholy blue, like a solitary royal figure.

Yet he never wearied of her: never, on leaving his love nest, and strolling joyfully down the pavement in the fresh morning air, did he feel that selfish pleasure of the cigar and the hands in the pockets of which our great modern novelist speaks somewhere.[2]

If he lacked a heart, Samuel had a noble intelligence, and, instead of ingratitude, pleasure had engendered in him that savoury contentment, that sensual reverie, which may well be worth more than love as the masses understand it. Moreover, La Fanfarlo had done her best and given him her most skilful caresses, having realized that the man was worth the trouble: she had grown used to his mystical language, laced with enormously crude expressions and impurities.—For her it had at least the attraction of novelty.

The dancer's sudden impulse had not passed unnoticed. The theatre poster had announced several cancellations; she had neglected rehearsals; many people were envious of Samuel.

One evening when chance, M. de Cosmelly's boredom, or a series of ruses on his wife's part had reunited them at the fireside—after one of those long silences which take place between couples who have little to say to each other and a great deal to hide from each other—after having made him the best tea in the world, in a very modest and very cracked tea pot, perhaps the very same that had been in her aunt's manor house—having sung for him at the piano a few pieces of music popular ten years ago—she said to him in the gentle and prudent voice of virtue which wants to make itself amiable and is afraid it might frighten off the object of its affections—that she greatly pitied him, that she had wept a great deal, even more for his sake than for her own; that, in her utterly submissive and entirely devoted resignation, she would at least have liked him to have found elsewhere than with her the love he no longer asked

[2] The author of *La Fille aux yeux d'or.* CB

of his wife; that she had suffered more from seeing him deceived than herself abandoned; that, moreover, she was greatly to blame, that she had neglected her duties as a tender spouse in not warning her husband that he was in danger; that, in addition, she was perfectly ready to close that bleeding wound and repair all alone an imprudent act they had both committed, etc.—and all that can be suggested in the way of honeyed words by a ruse authorized by love.—She wept and wept well; the fire lit her tears and her face embellished by grief.

M. de Cosmelly said not a word and went out. Men caught in the trap of their own faults do not like to offer their remorse to clemency. If he went to La Fanfarlo's house, he no doubt found there traces of disorder, cigar butts and articles.

One morning, Samuel was awakened by La Fanfarlo's rebellious voice and slowly lifted his weary head from the pillow on which it rested, to read a letter she handed to him:

'Thank you, sir, a thousand thanks; my happiness and my gratitude will be credited to you in a better world. I accept: I am taking my husband back from your hands, and am going with him this evening to our lands at C***, where, thanks to you, I shall recover my health and my life. Accept, sir, the promise of an eternal friendship. I have always believed you too honest a man not to prefer an extra friendship to any other reward.'

Samuel, sprawled on the lace, and leaning on one of the coolest and most beautiful shoulders one could set eyes on, had a vague feeling he had been duped, and had some difficulty in gathering together in his memory the elements of the plot of which he had brought about the conclusion; but he said calmly: 'Are our passions really sincere? who can be certain what he wants and who can know fully the barometer of his heart?'

'What are you muttering there? What is all this? I want to see,' said La Fanfarlo.

'Oh, nothing,' replied Samuel. 'A letter from an honest woman to whom I'd given a promise to make you love me.'

'You'll pay me for that.' she muttered under her breath.

It is probable that La Fanfarlo loved Samuel, but with that

love that few souls know, a love which has in its depths an element of rancour. As for him, his punishment fitted his crime. He had often aped passion; he was obliged to experience it; but it was not the tranquil love, the calm strong love that honest girls inspire; it was the terrible, distressing, and shameful love, the sickly love of courtesans. Samuel knew all the tortures of jealousy, and the humiliation and sadness into which we are thrown by the awareness of an incurable and constitutional evil—in a word, all the horrors of that vicious marriage known as concubinage.—As for her, she grows fatter by the day; she has become a plump, clean, gleaming, and cunning beauty, a kind of ministerial call girl.—One of these fine days she'll fast for Lent and give alms to her parish. At that stage, perhaps, Samuel, having died in harness, will be nailed down in his coffin, as he used to say in the good old days, and La Fanfarlo, with her canoness's bearing, will turn a young heir's head.—Meanwhile, she's learning to make children: she has just been delivered of a pair of healthy twins.—Samuel has given birth to four learned books: one book on the four evangelists—another on the symbolism of colours—a monograph about a new system of advertisements—and a fourth whose title I have no wish to recall. The most horrifying thing about this last book is that it is full of verve, energy, and curiosities. Samuel had the hide to give it the epigraph: *Auri sacra fames!** La Fanfarlo wants her lover to be a member of the Institute and is scheming at the Ministry to get him the cross.

Poor singer of *Ospreys*. Poor Manuela de Monteverde! How low he has fallen!—I learnt recently that he had founded a socialist newspaper and wanted to turn to politics.—What dishonest intelligence!—as the honest M. Nisard* says.

SHORT PROSE POEMS

To Arsène Houssaye*

My dear friend, I'm sending you a little piece of work of which it would be quite unjust to say that it has neither head nor tail, since everything, on the contrary, is both head and tail, alternatively and reciprocally. Just think what admirable advantages such a combination offers to everyone, to you, to me, and to the reader. We can interrupt wherever we wish, I, my reverie, you, the manuscript, the reader, his reading; for I am not tying a reader's recalcitrant will to the unending thread of a superfluous plot. Remove one vertebra, and the two halves of this tortuous fantasy will have no difficulty in reuniting. Chop it into a number of fragments and you will see that each can exist on its own. In the hope that some of these stumps will be lively enough to please and amuse you, I'm taking the liberty of dedicating to you the entire snake.

I have a small confession to make to you. It was in leafing through, for at least the twentieth time, Aloysius Bertrand's famous *Gaspard de la nuit** (doesn't a book known by you, by me, and by a few of our friends have every right to be called *famous*?) that I had the idea of attempting something similar, and applying to the description of modern life, or rather of *a* modern and more abstract life, the procedure he had applied to the depiction of ancient life, which is so strangely picturesque.

Who among us has not, in moments of ambition, dreamt of the miracle of a form of poetic prose, musical but without rhythm and rhyme, both supple and staccato enough to adapt itself to the lyrical movements of our souls, the undulating movements of our reveries, and the convulsive movements of our consciences?

This obsessive ideal springs above all from frequent contact with enormous cities, from the junction of their innumerable connections. Isn't it true that you yourself, my dear friend, have attempted to translate in a *song* the strident cry of the *Glazier,** and to express in lyrical prose all the distressing suggestions that cry sends to the very attics, through the highest fogs of the street?

But, to tell the truth, I fear my jealousy has not brought me happiness. No sooner had I begun my work than I realized not only that I remained very far from my mysterious and brilliant model, but also that I was doing something (if it can be called *something*) which was curiously different, an accident in which anyone but I would doubtless take pride, but which can bring only profound humiliation to a mind which considers the poet's greatest honour to lie in accomplishing *exactly* what he planned to do.

Your most affectionate,
C. B.

I *The Outsider*

'Whom do you love most, oh man of mystery? Tell me, is it your father, your mother, your sister, or your brother?'

'I have neither father nor mother, neither sister nor brother.'

'Your friends?'

'You're using a word whose meaning has to this day eluded me.'

'Your country?'

'I do not know in what latitude it lies.'

'Beauty?'

'Beauty I would love with all my heart, were she a goddess and immortal.'

'Money?'

'I hate it as you hate God.'

'Well! what do you love then, extraordinary outsider?'

'I love the clouds ... the clouds that pass by ... over there ... over there ... the marvellous clouds!'

II *The Old Woman's Despair**

The little old woman, wizened with age, was filled with delight on seeing the pretty child who was the focus of all attention, whom everyone wanted to please; this pretty creature, as fragile as she herself was, and, like her too, hairless and toothless.

And she came up to him, wanting to smile and simper at him.

But the horrified child struggled under the caresses of this decrepit old dear, and filled the house with his howling.

Then she withdrew into her eternal solitude and went off to weep in a corner, saying to herself: 'Alas, for us unfortunate old females, the time has passed when we could give pleasure, even to the innocent; and we bring only horror to the little children we want to love!'

III *The Artist's* Confiteor

How penetrating is the close of day in autumn! Oh! penetrating to the very point of pain, for there are certain delicious sensations, which, while imprecise, are not without intensity; and no blade has a keener tip than that of Infinity.

How great a delight it is to drown one's gaze in the vastness of sky and sea! The solitude, the silence, the incomparable chastity of all that azure! a small sail trembling on the horizon, imitating in its minuteness and its solitude my own irremediable existence, the monotonous melody of the surge, all these things think through me and I through them (for in the grandeur of reverie, the sense of self soon fades!);* they think, as I say, but in music and pictures, without quibbles, without syllogisms, without deductions.

And yet, these thoughts, whether they come from me or spring from objects, soon become too intense. When energy combines with sensual delight it creates a mental malaise and positive pain. My over-stretched nerves now produce only clamorous and painful vibrations.

And now the depth of the sky fills me with consternation; its clarity exasperates me. The insensitivity of the sea, the immutability of the spectacle revolt me ... Oh! must one endlessly suffer or endlessly flee from beauty? Nature, merciless enchantress, ever-victorious rival, let me be! Tempt no more my desires and my pride! The study of beauty is a duel in which the artist screams with fear before being defeated.

iv *A Prankster*

The New Year's celebrations were in full swing. A chaos of mud and snow, traversed by a thousand carriages, glittering with toys and sweets, bristling with greed and grief, a city's official delirium, destined to disturb the mind of the strongest recluse.

In the midst of this uproar and confusion, a donkey trotted briskly along, harassed by a whip-bearing lout.

As the donkey was about to turn the corner of a footpath, a handsome gentleman, gloved and polished, cruelly cravatted and imprisoned in brand new clothes, bowed ceremoniously to the humble beast, and said to him as he raised his hat: 'A happy and prosperous New Year to you!' Then he returned to his companions with a fatuous air, as if to ask them to crown his contentment with their approval.

The donkey did not see this fine prankster, and went on zealously trotting to wherever his duty called him.

As for me, I was suddenly seized with boundless rage at this magnificent imbecile, who seemed to me to concentrate within him all the wit of France.

v *The Double Bedroom*

A bedroom resembling a reverie, a bedroom which is truly *spiritual*, in which the stagnant atmosphere is faintly tinged with pink and blue.

There your soul can bathe in idleness, spiced with regret and desire.—It is something vaguely crepuscular, something bluish and pinkish; a dream of pleasure during an eclipse.

The furniture seems elongated, enervated, languid. The furniture seems to dream; it appears to be living in a state of trance, like the vegetable and mineral worlds. The materials speak a silent language, like the flowers, like the sky, like the setting sun.

On the walls no artistic abomination. Compared to the pure dream, compared to the unanalysed impression, definite art, positive art is blasphemy. Here everything possesses the necessary clarity and the delicious obscurity intrinsic to harmony.

An infinitesimal amount of the most exquisitely chosen perfume, combined with a very light humidity, floats in this atmosphere, where the drowsy spirit is lulled by sensations reminiscent of a conservatory.

Muslin falls in abundance before the windows and the bed; it billows out in snowy cascades. On this bed lies the Idol, the sovereign of dreams. But how does she come to be here? Who brought her? What magic power has installed her on this throne of reverie and pleasure? What does it matter? She is here! I recognize her.

Those really are the eyes whose flame pierces the dusk; those subtle and terrible *peepers* that I recognize because of their terrifying malice! They attract, they subjugate, they devour the gaze of anyone unwise enough to contemplate them. I have often studied them, those black stars which command curiosity and admiration.

To what benevolent demon am I indebted for being thus wrapped in mystery, silence, peace, and perfumes? O bliss! What we generally call life, even in its happiest expansions, has nothing in common with this supreme life that I now know about and that I savour minute by minute, second by second!

No, there are no more minutes, there are no more seconds! Time has disappeared. It is Eternity that reigns, an eternity of delights!

But a horrible blow, a heavy blow, resounded at the door, and, as in those infernal dreams, it seemed to me that I had received a mattock blow in the stomach.

And then a Spectre came in. A bailiff come to torture me in the name of the law; an infamous concubine come to bewail her fate and add the trivialities of her life to the suffering of my own; or a newspaper-editor's errand boy come to demand the next instalment of the manuscript.

The heavenly room, the idol, the sovereign of dreams, the *Sylphide* as the great René* used to say, has disappeared, all that magic swept away by the Spectre's brutal blow.

O horrors, I remember! I remember! Yes, this hovel, this abode of eternal boredom, is indeed my own. Here is the stupid furniture, dusty and down-at-heel; the fireplace with neither flame nor embers, soiled with spittle, the gloomy windows down which the rain has traced furrows in the dust; manuscripts, crossed out or incomplete; the calendar on which my pencil has marked the ill-starred days!

And that other-worldly perfume, which intoxicated my refined sensibilities, is replaced, alas!, by a fetid odour of tobacco mingled with an unidentifiable and nauseating mouldiness. Here one breathes in the stale air of desolation.

In this world, so narrow but so full of disgust, only one well-known object smiles at me: the phial of laudanum: a terrible old flame, and like all old flames, alas!, prodigal in caresses and treachery.

Ah yes! Time has reappeared; Time reigns as sovereign now; and with the hideous old man has returned all his demoniacal train of Memories, Regrets, Spasms, Fears, Anguish, Nightmares, Rages, and Neuroses.

I can assure you that now the seconds mark their passage strongly and solemnly, and each, as it leaps from the pendulum, says: 'I am Life, unbearable, implacable Life!'

There is only one Second in human life which has the mission of announcing good tidings, the only good tidings which cause each of us such inexplicable fear.

Yes, Time reigns; he has resumed his brutal dictatorship. And he drives me mad as if I were an ox, with his double goad. 'So toil, burro! Sweat, slave! Live, wretch!'

VI *To Each His Monster* *

Under a broad grey sky, on a broad dusty plain, devoid of paths, devoid of thistles, devoid of nettles, I met several men who were walking along with bowed backs.

Each of them bore on his back an enormous Monster, as heavy as a sack of flour or coal, or the paraphernalia of a Roman foot-soldier.

But the chimerical beast was not an immobile mass; on the contrary, it enveloped and oppressed each man with its powerful, elastic muscles; it clung with its two enormous claws to its bearer's chest; and its fabulous head rose above the man's brow like one of those horrendous helmets with which the warriors of antiquity hoped to increase their enemy's terror.

I questioned one of these men and asked him where they were going in this manner. He told me he knew nothing about it, and that the others were as much in the dark as he: but he added that they must be going somewhere, since they were driven by an irresistible desire to walk.

One curious thing should be noted: none of these travellers appeared irritated by the ferocious beast which hung from his neck and clung to his back; it seemed that they considered it as part of themselves. Not one of these weary and serious faces revealed any despair; under the splenetic bowl of the sky, their feet deep in the dust of a soil as desolate as that sky, they walked with the resigned expression of those condemned to hope forever.

And the procession passed by me and disappeared into the haze of the horizon, at the point where the rounded surface of the planet escapes from the curiosity of the human gaze.

And for a few instants I persisted in trying to understand this mystery; but soon unconquerable Indifference swooped down upon me and laid on me as heavy a burden as they themselves carried in the shape of their oppressive monsters.

VII *The Jester and the Goddess*

What an admirable day! The vast park swooned under the burning eye of the sun, as youth swoons under the domination of Love.

It was not through noise that the universal ecstasy of things found expression; the water itself appeared to sleep. Very different from human festivities, this was a silent orgy.

It seemed that a constantly growing light made the objects glitter more and more brightly; the excited flowers burnt with the longing to rival the blue of the sky through the energy of their own colours, and the heat, giving a visible form to perfumes, raised them up towards the planet as though they were wisps of smoke.

Nevertheless, in the midst of that universal delight, I noticed a grieving soul.

At the feet of a colossal Venus, one of those artificial jesters, one of those voluntary jokers whose task it is to make kings laugh when Remorse or Boredom obsesses them, decked out in a dazzling and ridiculous costume, with horns and bells on his head, crouched up against the pedestal and raised his tear-drenched eyes towards the immortal Goddess.

And his eyes said: 'I am the lowliest and most solitary of humans, deprived of love and friendship, and therefore far more lowly than the most imperfect of animals. Yet I, even I, have the capacity to understand and experience immortal Beauty. Oh! Goddess! Take pity on my sorrow and my frenzy!

But the implacable Venus gazed out at something in the far distance with her marble eyes.

VIII *The Dog and the Flask*

'My fine dog, my good dog, my dear little doggy, come here and breathe in an excellent perfume acquired from the best perfume-maker the city possesses.'

And the dog, wagging his tail, which is, I believe, the sign that, in these poor creatures, represents laughter and smiles, came closer and placed his moist nose curiously over the uncorked phial; then, suddenly springing back in fear, he barked at me reproachfully.

'Oh! you wretched dog! Had I offered you a parcel of dung you'd have sniffed at it in delight and would perhaps have devoured it. So even you, the unworthy companion of my drab life, are like the general public, who must never be given delicate scents, which only exasperate them, but instead carefully chosen ordure.'

IX *The Bad Glazier*

There exist certain individuals who are, by nature, given purely to contemplation and are utterly unsuited to action, and who, nevertheless, under a mysterious and unknown impulse, sometimes act with a speed which they themselves would have thought beyond them.

The sort of man who, for fear of finding that his caretaker has a distressing piece of news for him, prowls in cowardly fashion before his door for a whole hour before daring to go home; or the sort who keeps a letter for a fortnight before opening it, or who takes six months to resign himself to taking steps which have been necessary for a year; such men sometimes feel themselves suddenly hurled into action by an irresistible force, as if they were arrows shot from a bow. The moralist and the medical man, who claim to know everything, are unable to explain where these lazy and sensual souls find so abrupt a source of insane energy and how it is that they who are incapable of performing the most simple and necessary tasks discover at a particular moment an excess of courage to carry out the most absurd acts, acts which are often even highly dangerous.

One of my friends, the most inoffensive dreamer to have walked this earth, once set fire to a forest, to see, so he used to say, whether the flames took hold as easily as is generally claimed. Ten times in a row the experiment failed; but at the eleventh attempt it succeeded only too well.

Another will light up a cigar as he stands by a barrel of gunpowder, *to see, to know, to tempt fate*, to force himself to show that he does possess energy, to ape the gambler, to discover the pleasures of anxiety, for no real cause, through a whim, through having nothing else to do.

This is the kind of energy which springs from boredom and reverie; and those in whom this energy reveals itself so unexpectedly are, generally, as I've said, those most marked by indolence and a tendency to dream.

Another, so timid that he lowers his eyes even before the glances of men, so shy that he has to summon up all his poor will-power in order to go into a café or walk past a theatre box-office, where the ushers seem to him invested with the majesty of Minos, Aeacus, or Rhadamanthus,* will abruptly fling his arms around the neck of an old man who walks by him and enthusiastically embrace him before the astonished crowd.

—Why? Because ... because he felt an irresistible sympathy for those particular features? Perhaps; but it is more legitimate to suppose that he himself does not know why.

I have more than once been the victim of such crises and outbursts, which give credence to the belief that malicious Demons slip into our souls and make us carry out, unknown to us, their most absurd desires.

One morning I had awakened feeling surly, sad, weary from doing nothing, and driven, so it seemed to me, to do something great, to perform a remarkable feat; and, alas, I opened the window!

(Notice, I beg you, that the spirit of mystification, which in certain people springs not from work or planning but from a chance inspiration, plays a large role, if only because the desire is so ardent, in that mood termed hysterical by doctors and satanical by those who think rather more clearly than doctors, which pushes us unresisting towards a host of dangerous or unsuitable actions.)

The first person I saw in the street was a glass-pedlar whose harsh, discordant cry rose up to me through the heavy, dirty atmosphere of Paris. It would, moreover, be impossible for me to say why this poor man aroused in me a sense of hatred as sudden as it was despotic.

'Hey! You', and I shouted out to him to come up. Meanwhile I reflected, not without a degree of gaiety, that as my room was on the sixth floor and the stairway was very narrow, he would have some difficulty in performing this ascension and that there were many places where he could not fail to bump the edges of his fragile merchandise.

At last he appeared: I examined all his panes with great curiosity and said to him: 'Don't tell me you have no coloured panes! no panes which are pink or red or blue, no magic panes, no panes of paradise? Well, you're an impudent wretch! You dare wander about in the suburbs of the poor and you don't even have windows which let us see life through rose-coloured glasses!' And I pushed him roughly to the stairway, into which he stumbled, muttering as he went.

I went over to the balcony and snatched up a small pot of flowers, and when the man reappeared at the doorway, I dropped my missile perpendicularly down on the hooks of his pack; and as the shock of the blow threw him down backwards, the end result was that he crushed under his back all his poor ambulatory fortune, which made the startling noise of a crystal palace pulverised by lightning.

And, intoxicated by my act of madness, I shouted furiously to him: 'Let us see life as something beautiful! as something beautiful!'

These nervy pranks are not without peril, and one can often pay dearly for them. But what does eternal damnation matter to one who has found in a second an infinity of pleasure?

x *One O'Clock in the Morning*

Alone at last!! Now all that you can hear is the rumble of a few tardy and exhausted hackney cabs. For a few hours, we'll possess silence, if not repose. At last! The tyranny of the human face* has disappeared, and now I will suffer only at my own hands.

At last! So I am at last allowed to relax in a bath of darkness! First, double lock the door. It seems to me that that double turn of the key will increase my solitude and strengthen the barricades which currently separate me from the world.

Horrible life! Horrible city! Let's recapitulate the day's events: saw several men of letters, one of whom asked me if one could get to Russia by land (no doubt he took Russia for an island); argued generously with the editor of a review, who countered each objection with the words: 'This is the party of honest folk', which implies that all other papers are written by scoundrels; greeted twenty odd people, fifteen of whom were unknown to me; distributed an equal proportion of handshakes, and did so without taking the precaution of buying gloves; to kill time during a shower went up to see a female mountebank who asked me to design a costume for her as *Venustre*,* paid court to a theatre director who dismissed me with these words: 'You'd perhaps be well advised to approach Z; he's the heaviest, stupidest, and most famous of my writers. The two of you might achieve something together. See him and then we'll see'; boasted (why?) about several scurrilous acts I've never committed and pusillanimously denied several other misdeeds I performed with joy, delight in boasting, crimes against human dignity; refused to do a friend an easy service and gave a written recommendation to a complete ass; oof! is that the lot?

Annoyed with everyone, annoyed with myself, I would dearly like to make amends and feel a little pride during the silence and solitude of night. Souls of those I have loved, souls of those

I have sung, strengthen me, support me, drive far from me the lies and the corrupting vapours of this world and you, my Lord, grant me the grace to produce a few fine lines which will prove to myself that I am not the lowliest of men, that I am not inferior to those I despise!

XI *The Wild Woman and the Little Sweetheart*

'Truly, my dear, you weary me immeasurably and unpityingly; to hear you sigh anyone would think that your sufferings were worse than those of sixty-year-old gleaners or the old beggar women who gather crusts of bread at tavern doors.

If your sighs at least expressed remorse, they'd earn you some honour; but they merely convey the satiety of well-being and the weariness of repose. And then you're always pouring out a torrent of useless words: "Love me truly! I need it so much! Console me here, caress me there!" Look, I want to try to heal you and we may find the means of doing so, for a mere pittance, in the midst of festivities and without having to go very far.

Look very carefully, I beg you, at that solid iron cage behind which can be seen moving about, screaming like a soul in hell, shaking the bars like an orang-utan exacerbated by exile, imitating to perfection now the circular bounds of a tiger, now the mindless motion of a polar bear, that hairy monster whose form possesses a faint resemblance to your own.

That monster is one of those animals generally called "my angel!", that's to say, a woman.* The other monster, the one screaming at the top of his voice, a stick in his hand, is a husband. He has chained up his legitimate wife as if she were a beast, and he puts her on show in the suburbs, whenever there's a fair, with the permission of the magistrates, I need hardly add.

Pay close attention! See how greedily (and perhaps she's not pretending!) she rends asunder the live rabbits and the cheeping chickens thrown to her by her mahout. "Come now", he tells her, "You mustn't eat all you own in a single day", and, on uttering that piece of wisdom, he snatches her prey cruelly away from her, so that the trailing entrails cling for a moment to the teeth of the ferocious beast, of the woman, I should have said.

There! a good blow with the stick to calm her down, for she casts terrible glances of greedy longing at the food snatched from her. Great Gods! That stick isn't the sort used in comedies, did you hear it resound on the flesh, notwithstanding her false pelt. So now her eyes bulge from her head and she howls more *naturally*. In her rage, her whole body sparks, as iron does when you beat it.

Such are the marital customs of those two descendants of Adam and Eve, those creations of your hand, my God! That woman is without question unhappy, although after all, perhaps, the titillating pleasures of fame may not be unknown to her. There do exist misfortunes which are more incurable, misfortunes which have no compensating factors. But in the world into which she has been thrown, she has never had reason to believe that woman deserves a different fate.

Now, let's return to us, my precious. When one considers the hells in which this earth abounds, what do you expect me to think of your pretty little hell, for you lie only on materials as soft as your skin, you never eat meat which is not cooked, and your skilled servant takes care to cut the morsels up for you.

And what meaning can there be for me in all those little sighs that swell your perfumed bosom, my robust flirt? And all those affectations you've gleaned from books, and that indefatigable melancholy, made to inspire in the spectator a sentiment far removed from pity? Truly, I sometimes long to teach you what real misfortune is.

Looking like that, my delicate beauty, your feet in the mud and your eyes turned swooningly skywards, as if to ask the heavens for a prince, you would probably be taken for a young frog invoking the ideal. If you despise the joist (which is what I now am, as you know perfectly well), beware of the stork who will *seize you, munch you, and kill you at its pleasure.**

However much of a poet I may be, I'm not so great a dupe as you'd like to think me, and if you weary me too often with your *precious* snivelling, I'll treat you like a *wild woman*, or I'll throw you out of the window like an empty bottle.

XII *The Crowds*

Not everyone has the gift of taking a plunge into the multitude: there is an art to enjoying the crowd; and they alone can draw from the human race a feast of vitality on whom a fairy has bestowed, while they were in their cradles, a taste for disguise and masks, a hatred of home life, and a passion for travel.

Multitude and solitude: equal and interchangeable terms for the poet who is active and productive. Those who are not able to people their solitude are equally unable to be alone in a busy crowd.

The poet benefits from an incomparable privilege which allows him to be, at will, himself and others. Like those wandering souls in search of a body, he enters, when he so desires, into the character of each individual. For him alone, everything is vacant; and if certain places appear to be closed to him, that is because in his eyes they are not worth the bother of visiting.

The solitary and pensive stroller finds this universal communion extraordinarily intoxicating. He who finds it easy to espouse the crowd knows feverish pleasures which will be eternally denied to the selfish man, who is as tightly sealed as a strong box, or the lazy man, who is as self-contained as a mollusc. He makes his own all the professions, all the joys, and all the sufferings that chance presents to him.

What men call love is very small, very restricted, and very weak compared with this ineffable orgy, this holy prostitution of the soul which gives itself entirely, poetry and charity, to the unforeseen which reveals itself, to the unknown which happens along.

It is good from time to time to teach the fortunate of this world, if only to humiliate, momentarily, their stupid pride, that there are joys superior to their own, joys which are more immense and more delicate. Founders of colonies, pastors of peoples, missionary priests living in exile in the world's furthest corners, doubtless know something of this mysterious intoxication; and in the bosom of the vast family their genius has created for itself, they must sometimes laugh at those who pity them for a fate so troubled and an existence so chaste.

XIII The Widows

Vauvenargues* says that in public parks there are paths haunted principally by ambition that has not been achieved, by inventors whose stars were against them, by hopes of glory that have miscarried, by hearts that have been broken, by all those tumultuous and closed souls in whom there still growl the last sighs of a storm, and who withdraw far from the insolent gaze of the joyous and the idle. These shady retreats are the meeting places of those whom life has maimed.*

It is above all to these places that the poet and the philosopher love to direct their eager conjectures. There they are certain to find food for thought. For if there is a place they scorn to visit, as I intimated a moment ago, it is above all the joy of those who are rich. That turbulence in the void has nothing to attract them. On the contrary, they feel themselves irresistibly drawn to all that is weak, ruined, saddened, orphaned.

A skilled eye is never deceived in such matters. In features which are rigid or dejected, in eyes which are sunken and lacklustre, or glittering with the last glow of battle, in those deep and numerous furrows, in those slow steps or jerky strides, can immediately be deciphered countless tales of love deceived, of devotion misunderstood, of exertions unrewarded, of hunger and cold humbly and silently borne.

Have you sometimes seen widows on those lonely benches, poor widows? Whether in mourning or not, they are easily recognized. Moreover, there is always something lacking in the mourning clothes of the poor, an absence of harmony which makes them all the more distressing. The poor are forced to economize on their grief. The mourning of the rich is complete in every detail.

Which is the sadder and the more saddening of widows, the one who pulls by the hand a moppet with whom she cannot share her reverie, or the one who is completely alone? I do not know ... I once followed for hour after hour an old woman afflicted in this way. This particular widow, stiffly upright under a little, worn shawl, revealed in all her being a stoic pride.

It was clear that her absolute solitude condemned her to habits typical of an old bachelor, and the masculine nature of her behaviour added a mysterious piquancy to its austerity. She lunched in some miserable café, the Lord knows on what. I followed her to the public reading room; and for a long time I spied on her while she leafed through the gazettes with busy eyes, eyes once burnt by tears, for news which held for her a powerful personal interest.

At last, in the afternoon, under a charming autumn sky, one of those skies from which fall countless regrets and memories, she sat down, away from the crowds, in a far corner of a park, to listen to one of those concerts with which the music of the regiments brings pleasure to the people of Paris.

What I was witnessing was doubtless the little indulgence of that innocent old woman (or that purified old woman), the well-earned consolation for one of those heavy days without friendship, without conversation, without a moment's joy, with no one in whom to confide, which God had been dropping upon her, perhaps for many years!, three hundred and sixty-five times a year.

And here's another: I can never prevent myself from glancing, if not with universal sympathy at least with curiosity, at the crowd of pariahs who crowd around the barriers at a public concert. The orchestra sends through the night songs of festivities, songs of triumph, songs of pleasure. Dresses float and glitter, glances meet, the idle, weary from doing nothing, rock back and forth, feigning an indolent enjoyment of the music. Here there is nothing but riches and happiness; nothing which does not exude and inspire freedom from cares and the pleasure of enjoying life; nothing, apart from the sight of the rabble which in the far distance leans on the outer gates, seizing scot-free, at the whim of the wind, a shred of music, and watching the glittering furnace within.

It is always interesting to watch the reflection of the rich man's joy in the poor man's eye. But on that day, through the working-class crowd clad in smocks and calico, I caught sight of a being whose nobility made a striking contrast with all the surrounding coarseness.

She was tall, majestic, so noble in all her bearing that I cannot remember having seen her equal in the collections of aristocratic beauties of the past. A perfume of lofty virtue emanated from her entire being. Her face, grown sad and thin, was in perfect harmony with the full mourning in which she was clad. She too, like the crowd with which she mingled and which she did not see, turned a profound gaze on the luminous world, and listened while she gently nodded her head.

What an extraordinary sight! 'It cannot be', I said to myself, 'that her poverty, if indeed it is poverty, would admit of sordid penny-pinching. Such a noble face assures me of it. So why does she remain, of her own free will, in surroundings where she is obviously out of place?'

But as I walked curiously past her, I believed I could guess the reason. The tall widow held by the hand a child who was dressed in black as she herself was; however low the entrance price, that money may well have been enough to pay for one of the little being's needs, or better still for a luxury, a toy.

And she will have returned on foot, meditating and dreaming, alone, always alone; for children are turbulent and selfish, neither gentle nor patient; and they cannot even, like the pure animal, like a dog or a cat, act as confidant for solitary sorrows.

XIV *The Old Mountebank*

Everywhere the holiday crowd spread out, sprawled out, enjoyed itself. It was one of those grand occasions that mountebanks, and with them the acrobats, the men who live by showing animals, and those who live by peddling goods, look to, months in advance, to compensate them for the harsh times of the year.

On such days it seems to me that workers forget everything, pleasure and work alike; they become like children. For the little ones it's a holiday, it's the horror of school put off for twenty-four hours. For the grown-ups, it's an armistice signed with life's malevolent powers, a respite in the universal struggle and strife.

Even the society man and those engaged in spiritual tasks find it difficult to escape the influence of this popular jubilation. Willy-nilly they absorb their share of this atmosphere in which cares are forgotten. As for me, like any true Parisian, I never fail to inspect all the booths on parade at such festive moments.

There was indeed a formidable rivalry among them; they squalled, bellowed, and howled. It was a mixture of hawkers' cries, of thundering brass and exploding rockets. Acrobats and Simple Simons contorted faces burned and shrivelled by wind and rain and sun; with the nerve of actors sure of their skills, they threw off witticisms and jokes as heavy and solid in their comedy as those of Molière. The strong men, proud of their massive limbs, as low of brow and short of skull as orang-utans, lounged majestically in leotards which had been specially washed the day before. Dancing girls, as beautiful as fairies or princesses, leaped and cavorted under the glow of lanterns which filled their skirts with stars.

Wherever you looked there was nothing but light, dust, cries, joys, tumult; while one group spent, the other group earned, and each group was equally joyous. The children clung to their mothers' skirts begging for a stick of sugar, or clambered on to their fathers' shoulders to get a better view of a conjuror as resplendent as a god. And through everything there filtered, stronger than all the perfumes, that smell of frying which is like the incense of such festivities.

At the end, at the very furthest end of that row of booths as if, ashamed, he had exiled himself from all these splendours, I saw a poor mountebank, stooping, debilitated, decrepit, the ruin of a man, leaning back against one of the poles supporting his booth; a booth more wretched than that of the most degenerate savage; a booth where two stumps of candles, dripping and smoking, still shed too bright a light on all his indigence.

Everywhere there was joy, profit, debauchery; everywhere a firm promise of bread for the morrow; everywhere a frenetic explosion of vitality. But here was absolute poverty, poverty decked out, to turn the screw of horror, in comical rags, where the contrast sprang from necessity even more than skill. He was not laughing, the poor wretch! He was not weeping or dancing or gesticulating, or shouting; he sang no song, neither gay nor grieving, he made no plea. He stood silent and motionless. He had renounced all, he had abdicated. His destiny was fixed.

But what a deep, unforgettable glance he sent around the crowd and the lights, whose moving flood stopped a few steps away from his repulsive poverty! I felt my throat grasped by the terrible grip of hysteria and it seemed to me that my eyes were dimmed by those rebel tears which will not fall.

What could I do? What would be the use of asking the poor devil what curiosity, what wonder he had to show in those stinking shadows, behind his ragged curtain? In truth, I did not dare; and even if the reason for my timidity makes you laugh, I'll admit that I was afraid I'd humiliate him. At last I had summoned up the courage to drop some money on one of his planks as I walked by, hoping that he would guess my intention, when a great eddy of people, caused by some disturbance or other, dragged me far away from him.

And as I went home, obsessed by this vision, I tried to analyse my sudden grief, and I said to myself: I have just seen the image of the old man of letters who has outlived the generation he so brilliantly amused; the image of the old poet who has no friends, no family, no children, degraded by his poverty and by public ingratitude, and into whose booth the forgetful world no longer wishes to enter!

xv *The Cake*

I was travelling. The countryside in which I found myself was of a grandeur and a nobility no one could resist. At that moment something of that grandeur and nobility doubtless passed into my soul. My thoughts fluttered about with a lightness like that of the atmosphere; vulgar passions, such as hatred and profane love, now seemed to me as far off as the clouds which filed past at the bottom of the abysses beneath my feet; my soul seemed as vast and as pure as the enveloping bowl of the heavens; memories of earthly things were weakened and diminished by the time they reached my heart, like the sound of the bells tied to imperceptible animals which were grazing far, far away, on the slope of another mountain. On the little motionless lake, so immensely deep it seemed black, there sometimes passed the shadow of a cloud, like the reflection of the cloak of a winged giant flying through the skies. And I remember that that solemn and rare sensation which is caused by swift and utterly silent movement filled me with a joy mingled with fear. In a word, I felt, thanks to the inspiring beauty which surrounded me, perfectly at peace with myself and with the universe. I even believe that, in my perfect bliss and my complete oblivion of all earthly ills, I had reached the point of no longer finding so ridiculous those newspapers claiming that man is born good when the incorrigible physical envelope renewed its demands and I thought about compensating for the weariness and relieving the hunger caused by such a long climb. I took from my pocket a large piece of bread, a leather cup, and a bottle of a certain elixir that the pharmacists used to sell in those days to tourists and which could, when needed, be mixed with snow water.

I was tranquilly slicing my bread, when a very slight noise made me lift my eyes. In front of me stood a little, ragged creature, black and tousled; his hollow eyes, wild and seemingly supplicating, devoured the piece of bread. And I heard him sigh, in a low rough voice, the word: '*cake*'. I couldn't help laughing at the name with which he thought fit to honour my almost white bread, and I cut off a goodly slice and offered it to him. He approached slowly, his eyes never leaving the object he so desired: then, snatching the morsel up with his hand, he leapt back abruptly, as if he feared that my offer might not be sincere or that I might already be wishing I'd never made it.

But at that very instant he was bowled head over heels by another little savage, come from God knows where, and so perfectly like the first that he could have been taken for his twin brother. Together they rolled on the ground, quarrelling over the precious prey, neither, doubtless, wanting to sacrifice half of it for his brother's sake. The first, enraged, seized the second by the hair; the latter seized his ear between his teeth and spat out a bloody little scrap, uttering a superb local oath. The cake's legitimate owner tried to sink his little claws into the usurper's eyes; in his turn the other tried with all his might to strangle his adversary with one hand while with the other he attempted to slip the prize of the combat into his pocket. But, despair lending him new strength, the vanquished rose up again and sent the victor rolling on the ground with a head butt in the stomach. Why describe a hideous struggle which in truth lasted longer then their childish strength seemed to promise? The cake travelled from hand to hand and changed from pocket to pocket at every second; but alas! it also changed in size, and when at last, exhausted, gasping, bloodstained, they stopped because it was impossible to continue, there was no longer, if the truth be told, any cause for battle; the morsel of bread had disappeared, scattered into crumbs as small as the grains of sand with which it mingled.

This spectacle had cast a pall over the countryside as far as I was concerned, and the calm joy in which my soul had taken such delight before I caught sight of these small men had totally vanished; for long it grieved me, and I would constantly repeat to myself: 'So there is then a superb country where bread is called *cake* and is so rare a delicacy that it is enough to cause a war which is completely fratricidal!'

XVI *The Clock*

The Chinese can see the time in the eyes of cats.

One day a missionary, strolling in the suburbs of Nanking, realized that he had forgotten his watch and asked a little boy what time it was.

The urchin of the Celestial Empire hesitated at first; then, on second thoughts, answered: 'I'll tell you in a moment'. A few seconds later, he reappeared, holding in his arms a very fat cat, and looking at it, as the saying goes, in the whites of its eyes, he affirmed without the slightest hesitation: 'It's not quite noon'. Which was true.*

For my part, when I lean towards the beautiful Féline,* she who is so aptly named, she who is at once the honour of her sex, the pride of my heart, and the perfume of my mind, be it night or day, in full sunlight or dark shadow, in the depths of her adorable eyes I always distinctly see the time, always the same time, a vast solemn time as broad as space, a time not divided into minutes and seconds—a motionless time which is not marked on clocks and which is nevertheless as light as a sigh, as swift as a glance.

And if some importunate person were to disturb me while my eyes rest on this delicious clock, if some dishonest and intolerant Genie, some Demon of mishap were to say to me: 'What are you gazing at so carefully? What are you looking for in the eyes of that creature? Do you see the time there, you slothful and prodigal mortal?', I would unhesitatingly reply: 'Yes, I see the time; it is Eternity!'

Well, madam, isn't that a truly meritorious madrigal, as emphatic as you yourself are? In truth, I had so much pleasure embroidering this pretentious piece of gallantry, that I'll ask nothing from you in exchange.

XVII *A Hemisphere in a Head of Hair*

Let me breathe in for hours and hours on end the odour of your hair, let me plunge my whole face into your hair as a thirsty man plunges into the water of a stream, let me wave your hair in my hand like a scented handkerchief, and shake memories into the air.

If only you could know all I see! all I feel! all I hear in your hair! My soul soars on perfume as the souls of other men soar on music.

Your hair contains an entire dream, full of sails and masts; it contains vast seas whose monsoons carry me towards charming climes, where space is bluer and deeper, where the atmosphere is full of the perfume of fruit and leaves and human skin.

In the ocean of your hair I can glimpse a port alive with melancholy songs, vigorous men of all nationalities and ships of all types, silhouetting their fine and complex architecture against a vast sky, where basks eternal heat.

In the caresses of your hair I rediscover the languor of long hours passed on a divan, in the cabin of a fine ship, rocked by the imperceptible swell of the port, between pots of flowers and jugs of refreshing water.

In the blazing hearth of your hair I breathe the scent of tobacco mingled with opium and sugar; in the night of your hair, I see the infinite expanses of tropical skies glittering blue; on the downy banks of your hair how intoxicating are the combined odours of tar and musk and coconut oil.

Let me long bite your heavy black tresses. When I chew your elastic hair, your rebellious hair, I feel as if I am eating memories.

XVIII *The Invitation to a Journey*

There is a superb country, a land of Cockaigne, so it is said, which I dream of visiting with an old friend. An exceptional country, drowned in the fogs of our North, a land which could be called the West's Orient, Europe's China, so extensively has a warm and capricious fantasy flourished there, and so patiently and obstinately has that fantasy illustrated it with rare and delicate plants.

A true land of Cockaigne, where all is beautiful, rich, tranquil, decorous, where luxury delights in finding itself mirrored in order; where life is luxurious and sweet to breathe; from which is excluded all that is disordered, turbulent, and unforeseen; where happiness is wedded to silence; where the cuisine itself is simultaneously poetic, rich, and exciting; where everything resembles you, my dear angel.

You know that feverish illness that possesses us in times of cold misery, that nostalgia for a country one does not know, that anguished curiosity? There is a land that resembles you, where all is beautiful, rich, tranquil, and decorous, where fantasy has formed and embellished a western China, where life is sweet to breathe and happiness is wedded to silence. It's there we should go to live, it's there we should go to die!

Yes, it's there we should go and breathe, dream, and draw out the hours through the infinite variety of sensations. A musician has written the *Invitation to the Waltz*,* who will compose an *Invitation to the Journey*, which one could offer to the beloved, to the chosen sister?

Yes, it is in this atmosphere that it would be good to live— there, where the hours pass more slowly and contain more thoughts, where clocks ring out happiness with deeper and more meaningful solemnity.

On shining panels, or on gilded leather of a sombre richness, there live discreet paintings, blissfully happy, calm, and profound, like the souls of the artists who created them. The sunsets, which lend such rich colours to the dining room or the lounge, are filtered through beautiful materials or those high, finely worked windows, divided by lead bars into numerous compartments. The furniture is vast, strange, bizarre, and armed, like refined souls, with locks and secret compartments. Mirrors, metals, materials, wrought gold and earthenware play for the eyes a silent and mysterious symphony; and from all objects, from all corners, from gaps in drawers and from folds in material arises a curious perfume, redolent of Sumatra, a perfume which seems to be the apartment's very soul.

A true land of Cockaigne, I tell you, where all is rich, clean, and shining, like a clear conscience, like a magnificent panoply of pots and pans, like a splendid piece of worked gold, like brightly coloured jewellery! The world's treasures pour in, as if it were the house of a hard-working man who had fully earned the whole world's gratitude. A unique land, superior to all others, as Art is superior to Nature, where Nature is moulded anew by Dream, where it is corrected, embellished, remodelled.

Let them search and search, forever driving back the limits of their happiness, those alchemists of horticulture! Let them propose prizes of sixty or a hundred thousand florins for the one who resolves their ambitious problems! As for me, I have found my *black tulip* and my *blue dahlia*!*

Flower beyond compare, tulip discovered anew, allegorical dahlia, it's there, is it not, in that fine land, with its tranquillity and its reveries, that we should go to live and flourish? Wouldn't you be framed in your own analogy, wouldn't you see yourself reflected, to speak like the mystics, in your own *correspondence*?

Dreams! Always dreams! and the more ambitious and delicate the soul, the further those dreams remove it from what is possible. Each man carries within him his own dose of natural opium, ceaselessly secreted, unendingly renewed, and from the hour of our birth to that of our death, how many hours can we count that have been filled with positive pleasure, with actions planned in advance and performed with success? Shall we ever inhabit, shall we ever step into, this picture my mind has painted, this picture that resembles you?

Treasures, furniture, luxury, order, perfumes, miraculous flowers, all of that is you. And they, too, are you, those great rivers and tranquil canals. Those enormous ships that sail on them, weighed down with riches, ships from which rise the monotonous songs of the rigging, they are my thoughts slumbering or swaying on your breast. You lead them gently to the sea that is Infinity, reflecting the depths of the sky in the clarity of your fine soul; and when, weary of the waves and gorged with the goods of the Orient, they return to their home port, they are still my thoughts returning, enriched, from the Infinite to you.

XIX *The Poor Child's Toy*

I want to provide the image of an innocent form of entertainment. There are so few amusements that are beyond reproach!

When you go out in the morning with the firm intention of strolling along the highways, fill your pockets with little inventions costing a penny,—like the flat puppet worked by a single thread, or the farriers beating on an anvil, or the rider and his horse whose tail is a whistle—and in front of inns, or at the foot of trees, present them to the children you meet, children who are unknown to you and who are poor. You'll see their eyes grow immeasurably wide. At first they won't dare take them; they'll doubt their good fortune. Then their hands will rapidly snatch up the gift and they will take flight, like cats who go and eat far away from you the morsels you've given them, for they'll have learnt to have no faith in man.

On a highway, behind the gate of a vast garden, at the end of which could be discerned the white hues of a pretty manor house bathed in sunlight, was a beautiful, fresh child, clad in those country clothes that are so coquettish.

Luxury, freedom from cares, the habitual sight of riches make such children so pretty that one is tempted to consider them moulded of a different substance from the children of mediocrity and poverty.

Beside him, lying on the grass, was a splendid toy, as fresh as its owner, varnished, gilded, clad in a crimson cloak and covered with plumes and glass beads. But the child was taking no notice of his favourite toy, and this is what he was looking at:

On the other side of the gate, out on the roadway, among the nettles and thistles, was another child, dirty, sickly, soiled with soot, one of those pariah-kids in whom an impartial eye would discover beauty, as the eye of a connoisseur can divine an ideal painting underneath a layer of carriage varnish, if only the repugnant patina of poverty were washed away.

Through those symbolic bars separating the two worlds, the highroad and the manor house, the poor child showed the rich child his own toy, which the latter examined avidly, as a rare and unknown object. Now, this toy, which the little slattern was teasing, shaking, and waving about in a barred box, was a live rat! The parents, no doubt as a means of saving money, had found the toy in life itself.

And the two children laughed at one another fraternally, with teeth that were *equally* white.

XX *The Gifts of the Fairies*

The Fairies had assembled in great numbers, to carry out the distribution of the gifts to the new-born, those who had come into the world in the last twenty-four hours.

All these antique and capricious Sisters of Destiny, all these bizarre Mothers of joy and grief, were very different from one other; some seemed gloomy and bad-tempered, others appeared frolicsome and teasing; some were young and had always been young; some were old and had always been old.

All those fathers who believe in Fairies had come along, each bringing his new-born child in his arms.

The Gifts, the Faculties, the good Fortunes, the insuperable Circumstances, were piled up beside the court, like prizes on the podium on prize-giving day. What was special in this case was that the Gifts were not a reward for effort, but, entirely to the contrary, they were a grace granted to those who had not yet lived, a grace which could determine their destinies and become a source of unhappiness just as easily as a source of happiness.

The poor Fairies were very busy, for there were a large number seeking gifts, and the intermediary world, placed between man and God, is, like us, under the sway of the terrible law of Time and his infinite posterity, the Days, Hours, Minutes, and Seconds.

In truth they were as dazed as ministers when there is a session, or employees at the pawn shop when the advent of a national holiday authorizes free redemptions. I even believe that from time to time they glanced at the hand of the clock with as much impatience as human judges who, having presided since morning, cannot prevent themselves dreaming of their dinner, their family, and their beloved slippers. If, in supernatural justice, there is sometimes a degree of haste and chance, we shouldn't be surprised that the same thing sometimes happens in human justice. In that case, wouldn't we ourselves be unjust judges?

As a result, the day saw several blunders which could be considered as bizarre, were prudence, rather than caprice, the distinctive and eternal characteristic of Fairies.

Thus, the ability to exert a magnetic attraction over money was granted to the sole heir of a very rich family, who, not possessing the slightest sense of charity, nor any desire for the most visible goods of life, was later to find his millions prodigiously embarrassing.

Thus the love of Beauty and the gift of Poetry were given to the son of a grim old codger, a quarry-man by profession, who could in no way assist the faculties or ease the needs of his deplorable progeny.

I forgot to tell you that the distribution in these solemn cases allows for no appeal and no gift may be refused.

All the Fairies were getting to their feet, believing their task completed: for there remained not a single gift, no largesse at all to throw to all this human fry, when a good chap, a poor little shopkeeper, I believe, stood up and, grasping the nearest fairy by her dress of multi-coloured mist, cried out:

'Hey, Lady, you're forgetting us! There's still my little one! I don't want to have come for nothing.'

The Fairy might have been embarrassed, for there was absolutely *nothing* left. But she remembered just in time a law which is well known, although rarely applied, in the supernatural world, the world inhabited by those impalpable deities who are friendly to man, and often obliged to adapt themselves to his passions, such as the Fairies, the Gnomes, the Salamanders, the Sylphides and Sylphes, the Nixies, the Undins and Undines—I mean the law which grants the Fairies in a case like this, that's to say, if the gifts should run out, the ability to give one more, a supplementary and exceptional gift, always providing the fairy has the necessary imagination to create one immediately.

So the good Fairy replied, with aplomb befitting her rank: 'I give your son ... I give him ... the *Gift of pleasing*!'

'But how do you mean pleasing? pleasing? why should one want to please?', asked the little shopkeeper pigheadedly, for doubtless he was one of those very common reasoners who are incapable of rising to the logic of the Absurd.

'Because! just because!', replied the Fairy angrily, turning her back on him; and rejoining the procession of her companions, she said to them: 'What do you think of that vain little Frenchman, who wants to understand everything and who, having obtained for his son the best of gifts, still dares question and discuss that which admits of neither question or discussion?'

XXI *The Temptations, or Eros, Plutus,* and Glory*

Last night, two superb Satans and a no less extraordinary She-Devil climbed the mysterious stairs by which Hell assaults the weakness of sleeping men and communicates with us in secret. And they came and posed gloriously before me, standing as if on a podium. A sulphuric splendour emanated from these three individuals, highlighting them against the opaque backdrop of the night. They looked so proud and so imperious that I first took all three for real Gods.

The face of the first Satan was of indeterminate sex, and the lines of his body also possessed the softness of antiquity's statues of Bacchus. His beautiful languishing eyes, whose colour was shadowy and vague, recalled violets still weighed down with the heavy tears of the storm, and his half-open lips resembled those warm scent burners exhaling the good odour of a perfume shop. And each time he sighed, musk-bearing insects blazed as they fluttered about in the fire of his breath.

Around his crimson tunic was rolled, by way of a belt, a shimmering snake, which held its head erect and languorously gazed at him with its burning eyes. From this living belt hung, alternating with jars full of sinister liquids, glittering knives and surgical instruments. In his right hand he held another jar whose contents were of a luminous red, and which bore as its label these bizarre words: 'Drink, this is my blood, a perfect cordial.' In his left hand was a violin which he doubtless used to sing of his pleasures and pains and to spread the contagion of his madness on nights of Sabbath.

From his delicate ankles trailed a few rings of a broken gold chain and when the resultant awkwardness forced him to look down to the ground, he vainly contemplated his toe nails which were as shiny and polished as well-worked stones.

He gazed at me with eyes which were inconsolably sorrowful, eyes from which flowed an insidious intoxication, and he said to me in his sing-song voice: 'If you wish, if you wish, I'll make you lord of souls; and you'll hold sway over living matter, even more than the sculptor commands his clay; and you will know the endlessly renewed pleasure of leaving yourself to find oblivion in others and attracting other souls to yours, to the extent where they lose themselves in you.'

And I answered him: 'Thanks for nothing! I want no truck with that job lot of creatures who doubtless are no better than my own poor self. Whatever shame my memories bring me, I don't want to forget anything; and even if I did not know you, you old monster, your mysterious cutlery, your ambiguous jars, the chains in which your feet are caught, are symbols explaining pretty clearly the disadvantages of your friendship. Keep your presents.'

The second Satan had neither that simultaneously tragic and smiling air, nor those fine insinuating manners, nor that delicate, scented beauty. He was a vast man, with a plump eyeless face, whose heavy belly hung down over his thighs and whose skin was gilded and illustrated, as if by a kind of tattoo, with a mass of little figures which moved about and represented the numerous forms of universal suffering. There were little gaunt men, who, of their own volition, hung themselves from a nail; there were little misshapen, skinny gnomes, whose begging eyes, even more than their trembling hands, demanded alms; and then little old mothers holding stunted infants clinging to their exhausted breasts. There were many others still.

This fat Satan pounded his immense belly, whence issued forth a long and reverberating clanking of metal which ended in a vague moaning of numerous human voices. And he laughed, brazenly revealing his rotten teeth, with an enormous imbecilic laugh, like certain men the whole world over when they have dined too well.

And he said to me: 'What I can give you buys everything, is worth everything, replaces everything!' And he pounded his monstrous belly, whence a sonorous echo provided a commentary on his coarse expression.

I turned away in disgust and replied: 'My pleasure doesn't depend on anyone's suffering: and I have no desire for riches saddened, like wallpaper, with all the misfortunes represented on your skin.'

As for the She-Devil, I'd be lying if I did not admit that

at first sight I discovered in her a bizarre charm. To define that charm, I can think of no better point of comparison than that of beautiful women who are past their prime, but who no longer age and whose beauty retains the penetrating magic of ruins. She seemed both imperious and ungainly, and her eyes, although weary, exerted a spell-binding power. What struck me above all was the mysterious quality of her voice, in which I rediscovered the memory of the most delicious contraltos and also some of the huskiness of throats ceaselessly washed with brandy.

'Do you want to know my power?', said the false goddess in her charming and paradoxical voice. 'Listen.'

And then she lifted to her lips a gigantic trumpet, bedecked, like a toy flute, with ribbons proclaiming the titles of all the world's newspapers and through that trumpet she shouted my name, which thus rolled through space with the noise of a hundred thousand thunderclaps and returned to me reverberated by the echo of the furthest planet.

'Devil take it', I murmured, half under her yoke, 'now there's something worth having!' But when I examined the seductive virago more attentively, it seemed to me that I could vaguely remember having seen her drinking with a few jokers I know, and the raucous noise of the brass carried to my ears some indefinable memory of a prostituted trumpet.

And so I replied, summoning all my scorn: 'Away with you! I'm not the sort to marry the mistress of certain men I prefer not to name.'

Of course I had every right to feel proud of such courageous self-denial. But unfortunately I woke up and all my strength abandoned me. 'Truly', I said to myself, 'I must have been really heavily asleep to show such scruples. Oh! If only they could come back while I'm awake, I wouldn't be so fussy!'

And I invoked them loudly, begging them to pardon me, offering to dishonour myself as often as might be necessary to deserve their favours; but I must have offended them deeply, for they have never returned.

XXII *Evening Twilight*

Evening falls. A great sense of peace pervades poor spirits wearied by their day's labour; and their thoughts now assume the tender and indeterminate colours of dusk.

Nevertheless, from the mountain summit there descends to my balcony through the transparent clouds of evening a great howling, consisting of a mass of discordant cries, which the distance transforms into a lugubrious harmony, like that of the incoming tide, or of a rising storm.

Who are the ill-starred wretches for whom the evening does not bring calm, and who, like owls, take the coming of night for the signal of a witches' Sabbath? That sinister ululating comes to us from the black asylum perched on the mountain; and at evening as I smoke and contemplate the repose of the immense valley, bristling with houses each of whose windows proclaim: 'Peace is here now: here is the joy of the family!', I can, when the wind blows from the mountain, let those infernal harmonies lull my astonished mind.

Dusk stimulates the mad—I remember two friends of mine who were made quite ill by it. One of them would then disregard all the bonds of friendship and politeness, and savagely mistreat the first person he came across. I've seen him throw in the face of a head waiter an excellent chicken, in which he thought he'd detected Heaven alone knows what insulting hieroglyph. Evening, the forerunner of profound pleasures, spoiled the most succulent things for him.

The other, a man who had been wounded in his ambition, became, as evening fell, more bitter, more sombre, more trying. During daylight hours he was still indulgent and sociable, but in the evening he was merciless: and his wild, crepuscular madness directed itself not just towards others, but also towards himself.

The first died insane, unable to recognize his wife and child; the second carries within him the worry of a continual malaise and, were he to be granted all the honours republics and princes could confer upon him, I believe dusk would still kindle in his brain the burning desire for imaginary accolades. Night, which brought its darkness into their minds, brings light to mine, and although it is not unusual for one cause to engender two contrasting results, I am always somewhat intrigued and alarmed when it happens.

Oh night! Oh refreshing darkness! for me you signal an inner festival, you deliver me from anguish! In the solitude of the plains, in the stony labyrinths of a capital city, you, shimmering of stars, and you, explosion of lamps, you are fireworks celebrating the Goddess Liberty!

Dusk, how gentle and tender you are! The pink glow which still lingers on the horizon like day dying under the victorious oppression of its night, the flames of the candelabra glowing opaquely red against the final glory of the setting sun, the heavy drapes an invisible hand draws from the depths of the East, reflect all the complex feelings that struggle in the heart of man at the solemn moments of life.

Or you could compare it to one of those strange dresses a dancer wears, in which a dark, transparent gauze allows one to glimpse the muted splendours of a dazzling skirt, just as the blackness of the present is pierced by the delicious past; and the trembling stars of gold and silver, scattered all over it, represent those conflagrations of fantasy which catch fire properly only under the deep mourning of Night.

XXIII *Solitude*

A philanthropic journalist tells me solitude is bad for man, and in support of his claim he quotes, in the way of all unbelievers, the Fathers of the Church.

I know that the Devil delights in frequenting arid spots and that the Spirit of murder and lewdness flares up marvellously in lonely places. But it could be the case that such solitude is dangerous only for the idle and rambling mind which populates the desert with its own passions, its own hallucinations.

What is certain is that a chatterbox whose greatest delight consists in talking from the pulpit or the bench would run the highest risk of going completely mad on Robinson's island. I'm not asking of my journalist the courage and virtue of a Crusoe but I am asking him not to level any accusations at the lovers of solitude and mystery.

Our prattling races include individuals who would feel less reluctant to accept the final agony if, from the scaffold, they were allowed to harangue the crowds at length, with no fear of Santerre's* drums stopping them untimely in full cry.

I do not pity them, for I can see that their oratorical effusions bring them pleasures which are the equal of those that others find in silence and meditation. But I despise them.

My greatest wish is that my damned journalist would let me amuse myself in my own way. 'So you never feel the need', he asks me, giving his voice a very apostolic nasal tone, 'to share your pleasures?' You can see how subtle this envious man is! He knows I spurn his pleasures and he wants to worm his way into mine, the horrible spoil-sport!

'The great misfortune of not being able to be alone ...' La Bruyère* says somewhere or other, as if trying to shame all those who rush off to forget themselves in the crowd, fearing, no doubt, that they'll be unable to put up with their own company

'Almost all our misfortunes befall us as a result of our not having had the sense to stay in our room', says another sage, Pascal,* I think, thus recalling to the cell of meditation all those madmen who seek happiness in bustle and in a prostitution I could call 'brothertarian' if I wished to speak the fine language of the age I live in.

XXIV *Plans*

He was saying to himself as he strolled in a vast and solitary park. 'How lovely she would look dressed for the Court, in a complex, ornate gown, as, through the haze of a fine evening, she walked down the marble stairway of a palace, opposite vast lawns and ornamental ponds. For she possesses instinctively the grace of a princess.'

Later, as he walked along a street, he stopped in front of a shop selling engravings, and, finding in a folder a print which represented a tropical landscape, he said to himself: 'No! it's not in a palace that I want to possess her dear life. We wouldn't feel *at home*. Moreover, those gold-covered walls would leave no place to hang her picture. In those solemn galleries, there are no nooks allowing intimacy. Truly it's *there* that I ought to cultivate the dream of my life.'

And, as his eyes analysed the details of the print, his thoughts went on: 'Beside the sea, a beautiful wooden cabin overhung by those bizarre, glistening trees whose names have slipped my mind . . ., the atmosphere would be filled with an indefinable and intoxicating scent . . ., in the cabin a heady perfume of rose and musk . . . further off, behind our small domain, the tops of masts rocking on the ocean swell. The bedroom would be lit by a pink glow filtered through the blinds, it would be decorated with cool mats and heady flowers, with a few chairs in Portuguese rococo style, made of heavy dark wood (where she would rest so calmly, in such a pleasant breeze, smoking a tobacco lightly blended with opium!) and outside, beyond the verandah, the twittering of birds intoxicated with light, and the chatter of little Negresses . . . And at night, to accompany my reveries, the plaintive song of the music trees, the melancholy casuarinas. Yes, truly *this* is the scenery I was seeking. What have I to do with palaces?'

And further on, as he strolled along a fine avenue, he caught sight of a tidy little inn, from one of whose windows, brightened by curtains of gaily coloured calico, there leant out two laughing heads. And immediately he said to himself: 'My imagination must be a great wanderer to go so far in search of what is near at hand. Pleasure and happiness are in the first inn we come across, in the inn of chance acquaintances, so rich in pleasure. A roaring fire, brightly coloured crockery, a passable supper, a rough wine, and a very wide bed with sheets that may be somewhat coarse but which are clean. What could be better?'

And as he went home alone, at the hour when the voice of Wisdom is no longer silenced by the hum of external life, he said to himself: 'Today I have had, in imagination, three homes, each of which has given me equal pleasure. Why force my body to move from place to place, since my soul can travel so nimbly? And why turn plan into reality, when the plan is in itself sufficient pleasure?'

xxv *Beautiful Dorothea*

The sun crushes the town with its terrible, perpendicular light; the sand dazzles and the sea sparkles. The stupefied world spinelessly crumples and sleeps in a siesta which is a kind of pungent death, where the sleeper, half awake, savours the delight of being annihilated.

And yet Dorothea, as strong and proud as the sun, moves through the deserted street, the only living creature at this hour under the immense azure sky, forming against the sunlight a striking black silhouette.

She moves forward, with a soft swaying of her torso, which seems so slim against her broad hips. Her dress of clinging silk, in a light, pink colour, contrasts starkly with the darkness of her skin and moulds perfectly her deep waist, her hollow back, and her pointed breasts.

Her red sunshade, filtering the light, projects on to her dark face the blood-red rouge of its reflections.

The weight of her massive hair, so black that it's almost blue, pulls her delicate head backwards and makes her appear triumphant and indolent. Heavy pendants babble secretly as they hang from her dainty ears.

From time to time the sea breeze lifts her floating skirt up by a corner and reveals a gleaming and superb leg; and her foot, the equal of those on the marble goddesses that Europe shuts away in its museums, faithfully leaves its imprint on the fine sand. For Dorothea is so prodigiously flirtatious that the pleasure she feels in being admired triumphs over the pride she takes in having been freed, and although she is no longer a slave, she walks without shoes.

Thus she walks, harmoniously, happy to be alive and smiling an empty smile, as if she perceived in the far distance a mirror which reflected her gait and her beauty.

At an hour when the very dogs groan with pain under the

biting sun, what powerful reason drives our lazy Dorothea abroad, she who is as beautiful and cold as bronze?

Why has she left her little hut in which everything is so coquettishly arranged, in which flowers and mats create at so little expense a perfect boudoir, and in which she takes such pleasure in combing her hair, in smoking, in being fanned, or in looking at herself in the mirror of her great feather fans, while the sea which beats against the beach some hundred metres away, provides a powerful and monotonous accompaniment for her vague reveries, and the iron saucepan, in which there bubbles a stew of crab in rice and saffron, wafts from the back of the courtyard its stimulating scents?

Perhaps she has a meeting with some young officer who, on far-off beaches, has heard his comrades talk of the famous Dorothea. Without fail the simple creature will beg him to describe to her the Opera ball, and will ask him if you can attend in bare feet, as you do at the Sunday dances where the old Kaffir women themselves grow drunk and mad with joy; and then she'll ask him, too, if the lovely ladies of Paris are all more lovely than she.

Dorothea is admired and pampered by all, and she would be perfectly happy were she not obliged to pile up piastra on piastra to buy back her little sister who is fully eleven years old and who is already mature and so beautiful! She will succeed, no doubt, our good Dorothea; the child's master is so greedy, too greedy to understand a beauty other than that of money!

XXVI The Eyes of the Poor

Oh! so you want to know why I hate you today. No doubt it will be harder for you to understand than for me to tell you why; for you are, so I believe, the finest example of feminine impenetrability one could ever come across.

We had just spent in each other's company a long day which to me had appeared short. We had indeed promised each other that we would share all our thoughts and that henceforth our two souls would be as one a dream which has nothing original in it, after all, save that, although all men have dreamt it, none has realized it.

That evening you were somewhat weary and wanted to sit down on the terrace of a new café on the corner of a new boulevard, still full of rubble but already showing the glory of its unfinished splendours. The café sparkled. The gaslight itself lavished all the intensity of a première, and illuminated with all its might the blindingly white walls, the dazzling expanse of mirrors, the gold of the beading and corner-pieces, the plump-cheeked page-boys pulled along by dogs straining at the lead, ladies laughing at the falcon perched on their wrists, the nymphs and goddesses bearing fruit and meats and game on their heads, the Hebes and the Ganymedes stretching out their arms to offer the little jars of mousse or the bicoloured obelisks of mixed ice-creams; all history and all mythology placed at the service of gluttony.

Right in front of us, on the roadway, stood a good chap of about forty, his face weary, his beard streaked with grey, one hand holding a little boy, while he carried on his other arm a little creature too weak to walk. He was performing the function of a nanny and taking his children for an evening stroll. All were in rags. These three faces were extraordinarily serious, and their six eyes stared unwinkingly at the new café, all revealing the same degree of admiration, although their different ages introduced different shades of wonder.

The father's eyes said: 'How beautiful it is! how beautiful! You'd say that all the gold of the poor had gathered on those walls.' The eyes of the little boy: 'How beautiful it is! how beautiful! But it's a house you can go in only if you're not like us.' As for the eyes of the littlest one, they were too bewitched to express anything but a boundless and mindless joy.

The song-writers tell us that pleasure makes souls grow benevolent and hearts grow soft. The song got it right that evening, as far as I was concerned. Not only was I moved by that family of eyes, but I felt a trifle ashamed of our glasses and our jugs, which were bigger than our thirst. I turned my eyes to yours, oh my beloved, to read in them *my* thoughts; I was diving into your eyes which are so lovely and so strangely gentle, into your green eyes inhabited by Caprice and inspired by the Moon, when you said to me: 'I can't bear those people with their eyes as wide open as coal bunkers! Couldn't you ask the head waiter to send them on their way?'

So difficult it is to understand one another, my dear angel, and so hard it is for thoughts to be communicated, even between people who love each other!

XXVII *A Hero's Death*

Fancioulle* was an admirable clown, and almost one of the Prince's friends. But those devoted by their calling to the comic are often fatally attracted to serious matters, and although it may seem bizarre to suggest that ideas concerning Fatherland and Liberty could despotically seize hold of a comedian's mind, one day Fancioulle became a member of a conspiracy formed by several discontented noblemen.

There exist the world over upright men who will denounce to the powers that be individuals of a bilious humour who wish to depose princes and, without consultation, give a society a sea change. The gentlemen in question were arrested, as was Fancioulle, and condemned to certain death.

I would willingly believe that the Prince was almost annoyed to find his favourite comedian among the rebels. The Prince was neither better nor worse than his fellows; but his excessive sensitivity made him in many cases more cruel and more despotic than all his peers. A passionate lover of the fine arts, and moreover an excellent connoisseur, he could truly never have enough of pleasure. Fairly indifferent, where men and morals were concerned, a real artist in his own right, he knew no more dangerous enemy than Boredom, and the bizarre attempts he made to avoid or defeat this tyrant of the world would certainly have led a severe historian to apply to him the term 'monster', had it been permitted in his domains to write anything at all which did not have as its sole aim pleasure and astonishment, for astonishment is one of the most delicate forms of pleasure. It was this Prince's great misfortune that he never had a theatre vast enough for his genius. 'There are young Neros who are stifled by limits which are too narrow for them, leaving the ages to come forever ignorant of their names and their good will. Improvident Providence had given this Prince faculties far in excess of his estates.

Suddenly the rumour circulated that the sovereign wished to pardon all the conspirators; a rumour sparked off by the announcement of a great show in which Fancioulle was to perform one of his best and greatest roles. The show would even be attended, so it was said, by the condemned noblemen; an obvious sign, added superficial minds, that the Prince was minded to be generous.

From so naturally and so voluntarily eccentric a man, all was possible, even virtue, even clemency, particularly if he could hope to find in it unexpected pleasures. But for those who, like me, had been able to penetrate more deeply into that curious, diseased soul, it was infinitely more likely that the Prince wanted to gauge the value of the theatrical talents of a man condemned to death. He wanted to seize the opportunity to carry out a physiological experiment of *capital* interest and to ascertain the extent to which the normal ability of an artist could be altered or modified by the extraordinary situation in which he found himself; beyond that, was there in his soul a more or less clearly defined intention to be merciful? That is a point on which no one has ever been able to shed any light.

At last the great day dawned and the little court displayed all its pomp and splendour. It would be difficult to imagine, if you hadn't seen it, all the splendours the favoured class of a small State with limited resources is able to reveal on a truly solemn occasion. This occasion was doubly solemn, firstly because of the magical luxury displayed, and then because of the moral and mysterious interest attached to it.

Master Fancioulle excelled above all in those roles which are silent or in which few words are spoken, and which are often the leading parts in those fairy-tale plays whose aim is to represent in symbolic fashion the mystery of life. He came on stage lightly and with perfect self-possession, a fact which helped to strengthen in the noble public the idea of gentleness and pardon.

When you say of an actor: 'Now there's a good actor', you're using an expression which implies that beneath the character you can still perceive the actor, by which I mean artistry, effort, will-power. Now, if an actor succeeded in creating with the character whom it is his duty to represent a relationship parallel to that which the finest statues of Antiquity, if a miracle enabled them to live, walk, and see, would have with the general and vague idea of Beauty, that would doubtless offer a singular and entirely novel case. Fancioulle, that evening, was a perfect representation of the ideal, one you could not believe incapable of existing in reality. This clown walked to and fro, was convulsed with laughter or tears, and did all this with an indestructible halo around his head, a halo invisible to all but visible to me, and in which were mingled, in a strange amalgam, the rays of Art and the glory of Martyrdom. Fancioulle, through God alone knows what special grace, introduced the divine and the supernatural even into his most extravagant clowning. My pen trembles and tears of an ever-present emotion spring into my eyes as I attempt to describe for you this unforgettable evening. Fancioulle proved to me, in a manner at once peremptory and irrefutable, that the intoxication of Art is better able than any other to veil the terrors of the void; he proved that genius can perform comedy on the edge of the tomb with a joy that prevents him from seeing the tomb, lost, as he is, in a paradise which excludes all thought of tombs and destruction.

The entire audience, however blasé and frivolous it might have been, was soon under the all-powerful domination of the artist. No one dreamt any longer of death, of mourning, of torture. All of them abandoned themselves, unconcerned, to the multifarious delights caused by the sight of a masterpiece of living art. On several occasions explosions of joy and admiration shook the vaults of the edifice with the energy of continuous thunder. The Prince himself, intoxicated, joined in the applause of his court.

And yet, to clear-sighted eyes, his own intoxication was not unalloyed. Did he feel defeated in his power as despot?

Humiliated in the art of terrifying hearts and dulling minds? Frustrated in his hopes and shaken in his predictions? Such conjectures, although not exactly justified, while not absolutely unjustifiable, crossed my mind while I contemplated the Prince's face, on which a new pallor was constantly added to his habitual pallor, as snow is added to snow. His lips grew tighter and tighter and his eyes blazed with an inner fire which resembled that of jealousy and rancour, even while ostensibly he applauded the talents of his old friend, the strange clown who was clowning so brilliantly about death. At a certain moment, I saw His Highness lean towards a little page who was standing behind him and whisper something. The impish expression of the pretty child lit up in a smile; and then he swiftly left the Prince's box as if to carry out an urgent task.

A few minutes later a sharp, prolonged whistle interrupted Fancioulle in the middle of one of his best moments, and tore both ears and hearts asunder. And from the place in the theatre where this unexpected sign of disapproval had arisen a child rushed into a corridor with stifled giggles.

Fancioulle, shaken, woken in mid-dream, at first closed his eyes, then almost immediately opened them again, enormously wide, then opened his mouth as if to breathe in convulsively, staggered forward a little, then back a little, and then fell dead on the boards.

Had that dagger-swift whistle really deprived the executioner of his task? Had the Prince himself guessed how murderously efficient his trick would be? It is permissible to doubt that he had. Did he miss his dear and inimitable Fancioulle? It is sweet and legitimate to believe that he did.

The guilty noblemen had enjoyed the spectacle of comedy for the last time. On that very night they were dispatched from this world.

Since that time several mime artists, rightly valued in various countries, have come to perform before the Court of ***; but none of them has been able to bring back the wondrous talents of Fancioulle, nor to rise to the same *favour*.

XXVIII *The Counterfeit Coin*

As we were walking away from the tobacco shop, my friend carefully picked over his change; into his left waistcoat pocket he slipped small gold coins; in the right, small silver coins; in his left trouser pocket, a pile of brass coins and finally in the right trouser pocket a two-franc silver coin he had examined with special attention.

'Now that's a curious and careful division', I said to myself.

We met a pauper who held out his cap with trembling hands—I know nothing more disturbing than the silent eloquence of those begging eyes which contain, for those sensitive enough to read what they have to say, both a world of humility and a world of reproach. In them can be found something like that depth of complex feeling revealed by the tearful eyes of dogs that are being whipped.

My friend's offering was much greater than mine and I said to him: 'You're right; apart from the pleasure of being astonished, there's no greater pleasure than giving someone else a surprise.'

'It was the counterfeit coin', he replied calmly, as if to justify his prodigality.

But into my wretched brain, which is always trying to complicate matters (for such is the fatiguing faculty Nature has bestowed on me!) there suddenly came the idea that such behaviour, on the part of my friend, could be excused only by a desire to create an event in that poor devil's life, perhaps even to discover the diverse consequences, be they disastrous or otherwise, that can result from the presence of a counterfeit coin in the hand of a beggar. Could it not multiply in the form of real coins? Could it not also lead him to prison? An inn-keeper or a baker, for instance, would perhaps have him arrested either for making or for passing counterfeit coins. But it was equally likely that the false coin could provide a poor little speculator with the seeds of a few days' riches. And so my imagination wandered along, lending wings to my friend's mind and drawing all possible deductions from all possible hypotheses.

But my friend burst in upon my reverie by taking up my own words: 'Yes, you're right; there's no sweeter pleasure than that of surprising a man by giving him more than he hopes for.'

I looked him in the whites of his eyes and was horrified to see that those eyes shone with unquestionable candour. Then it dawned on me that he had sought to perform both an act of charity and a piece of good business, to win forty sous and the heart of God, to buy a cheap entrance into paradise, and finally to gain free and for nothing the reputation of being a charitable man. I would almost have forgiven him the desire for a criminal pleasure of which I had just a moment ago thought him capable; I would have considered it curious and bizarre that he amused himself by compromising the poor, but I will never pardon him for the bumbling nature of his calculations. There can never be any excuse for being wicked, but there is some merit in knowing that one is being wicked; and the most irreparable of vices consists in doing evil through stupidity.

XXIX *The Generous Gambler*

Yesterday, amidst the crowds on the boulevard, I felt myself brushed against by a mysterious Being whom I had always longed to know and whom I recognized immediately, although I had never seen him. He no doubt nurtured a similar desire where I was concerned for as he passed by he gave me a meaningful wink which I hastened to obey. I followed him attentively, and before long I followed him down into a dazzling underground dwelling, which glittered with a degree of luxury that none of the better Parisian abodes could come anywhere near equalling. It struck me as strange that I could so frequently have passed by this prestigious retreat without guessing the entrance to it. In that dwelling there reigned an exquisite, though heady, atmosphere, which made one forget almost instantaneously all the tiresome horrors of life; there one breathed in a sombre beatitude, like that which the lotus-eaters must have experienced when, setting foot on an enchanted island, lit by the glow of an eternal afternoon, they felt arise within them, to the soothing sounds of melodious cascades, the longing to see no more their homes, their wives, their children, and never to return again to the sea's soaring breakers.*

There you could see strange faces of men and women marked by a fatal beauty which I felt I had seen already at times and in countries which I was incapable of recalling exactly and which inspired within me more a fraternal sympathy than that fear which usually arises from the sight of the unknown. Were I to try to find some way of defining the singular expression of their gaze, I would say I had never seen eyes gleaming more energetically with the horror of boredom and the undying desire to feel themselves alive.

By the time we sat down, my host and I were already old and perfect friends. We ate, and we drank exorbitantly all manner of extraordinary wines, and, what is no less extraordinary, it seemed to me, after several hours, that I was no more drunk than he was. Meanwhile, gambling, that superhuman pleasure, had from time to time interrupted our frequent libations and I have to confess that I had gambled on my soul and lost it with heroic insouciance and lightness of heart. The soul is so impalpable, so often useless, and sometimes such a nuisance, that I felt no more emotion on losing it than if, on a stroll, I had mislaid my visiting card.

We spent a long time smoking a few cigars whose incomparable savour and perfume left in our hearts a sense of nostalgia for countries and joys we had not known, and, intoxicated with all these delights, I seized a brimming goblet and dared to shout, in an outburst of familiarity which did not seem to displease him. 'To your immortal health, old Cloven Hoof!'

We also chatted about the universe, its creation and its future destruction; about the great idea of the age, by which I mean progress and perfectibility, and in general of all forms of human infatuation. On that subject, His Highness poured out an unending flow of light-hearted and irrefutable jokes, and expressed himself with a smoothness of diction and a tranquil drollery that I have never found in the most celebrated human conversationalists. He explained to me the absurdity of the different philosophies which have, until now, taken hold of the human mind and even deigned to confide in me a few fundamental principles, the benefits and ownership of which it would not be fitting for me to share with anyone at all. He made no complaint whatsoever about the bad reputation he had attracted throughout the world, assured me that he himself was the person most concerned by the destruction of *superstition*, and admitted to me that as far as his own power was concerned he had been afraid on only one occasion, which was when he had heard a preacher, more subtle than his colleagues, shout out from the pulpit:

'Dearly beloved, never forget, when you hear anyone vaunt the progress of enlightenment, that the Devil's finest trick is to persuade you that he does not exist!'

The memory of that famous orator led us naturally to the subject of academies and my strange host assured me that in many cases he didn't disdain to inspire the pen, the page, and the conscience of teachers, and that he almost always attended in person, although invisible, all academic gatherings.

Encouraged by so much kindness, I asked him if he had any news of God, and if he'd seen him recently. He replied, with a carelessness tinged with a certain sadness: 'We bow to each other when we meet, like two old noblemen, in whom an innate politeness cannot completely stifle the memory of former resentment.'*

It is doubtful whether His Highness has ever given so long an audience to a simple mortal and I was afraid I might be abusing his goodwill. Finally, as shivering dawn whitened the window panes, this famous person, sung by so many poets and served by so many philosophers who work for his glory unawares, said to me: 'I want you to have good memories of me, and I'd like to prove to you that I, of whom so much ill is spoken, am sometimes a *good old devil*, to use one of your everyday expressions. To make up for the irremediable loss of your soul, I'll give you the prize you would have gained if fate had been on your side, that is, the ability to soothe and defeat throughout your entire life that strange disease of Boredom which is the source of all your illnesses and all your wretched progress. Never will you form a desire without my helping you to achieve it; you will reign over your common fellow men; you will be provided with flattery and even adoration; silver, gold, diamonds, and fairy-tale palaces will come to seek you out and beg you to accept them without your having to make any effort to win them; you will change country as often as your fancy decrees; you will grow drunk on pleasure and never weary of it, in charming lands where the weather is always warm and where the women smell as sweet as flowers,—et cetera, et cetera . . .', he added, rising and dismissing me with a kind smile.

Had I not been afraid to humiliate myself before so great a gathering I would willingly have fallen at the feet of this generous gambler, to thank him for such unheard-of munificence. But little by little, after I'd left him, my incurable distrust returned to me; I no longer dared to believe in such prodigious good fortune and, as I went to bed, saying my prayers through a remnant of imbecilic habit, I repeated half-asleep: 'My God! Lord, my God, make the devil keep his promise to me!'

xxx The Rope
For Édouard Manet*

'Illusions', my friend was saying to me, 'may be as innumerable as the relationships which bind one person to another, or those which link men to objects. And when the illusion disappears, that's to say, when we see the being or the fact as it exists outside us, we experience a bizarre sensation, rendered more complex partly by regret for the ghost we have lost and partly by agreeable surprise at the novelty, at the real fact. If ever there were an obvious and mundane phenomenon, one which is always the same and whose nature admits of no mistake, that phenomenon must be maternal love. It is as hard to imagine a mother without maternal love as it would be to picture a light without heat; so isn't it perfectly legitimate to attribute to maternal love everything a mother says and does where her child is concerned? And yet, let me tell you a little story which shows how strangely mystified I was by the most natural of illusions.

My profession as a painter drives me to cast an attentive
eye at the faces and physiognomies that I come across, and
you know what pleasure we extract from this gift, which makes
life appear to us more lively and significant than to other people.
In the remote suburb I live in, where the buildings are still
separated from each other by vast grassy expanses, I frequently
observed a child whose ardent and cheeky features instantly
attracted me more than all the others I saw. He posed for
me on more than one occasion and I transformed him some-
times into a little Gypsy, sometimes an angel, sometimes a
mythological Cupid. I made him carry the vagabond's violin,
the Crown of Thorns and the Nails of the Passion, and the
Torch of Eros. At length I took such a lively pleasure in this
lad and all his funniness, that one day I begged his parents,
who were poor, to be so kind as to let me have him, promising
that I would dress him well, give him a little money, and not
make him do anything more arduous than clean my brushes
and run messages for me. This child, once scrubbed clean,
became charming, and the life he led at my place seemed to
him to be paradise, compared with what he would have had
to put up with in his parents' hovel. Only I have to say that
this little chap sometimes astonished me with strange crises of
precocious sadness and that he soon revealed an immoderate
taste for sugar and liqueurs; with the result that one day when
I realized that, despite my numerous warnings, he had com-
mitted yet another theft of this sort, I threatened to send him
back to his parents. Then I went out and my business kept
me away from my home for a fairly long time.

Imagine my horror and astonishment when, on returning
home, the first object I set eyes on was my little lad, the cheeky
companion of my life, hanging from a panel of this very ward-
robe! His feet almost reached the floor; a chair, which he had
doubtless kicked aside, was overturned beside him; his head
hung convulsively on his shoulder; his swollen face and his wide-
open eyes, which stared with horrible steadiness, at first deluded
me into thinking that he was still alive. Getting him down was
not as easy a task as you might imagine. He was already very
stiff and I felt an inexplicable repugnance at the thought of

letting him fall roughly to the floor. I had to support his entire
weight with one arm, while I cut the rope with my other hand.
But even when that was done, it wasn't over; the little monster
had used a very thin cord which had bitten deeply into the
neck and I now had to use a pair of small scissors to find the
thread between the two rolls of swollen flesh so I could free
his throat.

I forgot to tell you that I had shouted loudly for help; but
all my neighbours had refused to come to my aid, remaining
true to the habits of civilised man, who is never willing, I can't
imagine why, to get mixed up in anything to do with anyone
who has hanged himself. At last there came a doctor who de-
clared that the child had been dead for several hours. Later
when we had to undress him for the burial, the rigidity of the
corpse was such that we could not bend his limbs and had
to tear and cut the clothes in order to remove them from him.

The Chief Constable, to whom, of course, I had to declare
the accident, cast me a sideways glance and said to me: "This
is all a bit murky!", moved, no doubt, by an inveterate desire
and a professional habit of frightening, just on the off chance,
innocent and guilty people alike.

There still remained one supreme task to fulfil, the mere
thought of which caused me terrible anguish; the parents had
to be informed. My feet refused to carry me there. At last
I summoned up courage. But, to my great surprise, the mother
was unmoved, not a single tear gathered at the corner of her
eye. I attributed this strange fact to the very horror she must
be experiencing and remembered a well-known expression:
"The most terrible grief is that which is silent." As for the
father, he merely mumbled, half crushed, half thoughtful: "After
all, perhaps it's better like this; he would have come to a bad
end in any case!"

Meanwhile the corpse was still stretched out on my divan,
and, with the aid of a maidservant, I was making the final
preparations, when the mother came into my studio. She
wanted, so she said, to see her son's body. In truth, I could
not prevent her from drowning herself in grief by refusing her
this supreme and sombre consolation. Finally she begged me

to show her the place where her little one had hanged himself. "Oh, no", I answered, "That would be far too upsetting for you!" And as my eyes involuntarily turned towards the fatal wardrobe, I realized, with a mixture of disgust, horror, and anger, that the nail had remained in the panel with a long piece of rope still hanging from it. I leapt swiftly forward to tear down these last vestiges of the accident, and as I was about to hurl them through the open window, the poor woman grasped my arm and said to me in irresistible tones: "Oh! let me have that! I beg and beseech you!" Doubtless her despair, or so it seemed to me, had driven her so mad that she was now filled with tenderness on seeing the instrument of her son's death and she wanted to keep it as a horrible and beloved relic. She seized the nail and the rope.

At last! At last all was done. All I had to do now was to go back to work, more eagerly than usual, to drive away little by little this small corpse which haunted the recesses of my mind and whose ghost wearied me with its large staring eyes. But the next day I received a pile of letters: some, from lodgers in the house, others from people in neighbouring houses; one from the first floor; another from the second; yet another from the third, and so on, some half-jocular, as if attempting to disguise the sincerity of their request under apparent banter, while others, coarsely unashamed and badly spelled, but all with the same aim in mind, that is, in the hope of obtaining a piece of the deadly and blessed rope. Among the signatories there were, I must confess, more women than men; but not all, take my word for it, belonged to the lowest and basest class. I kept the letters.

And then, suddenly, a flash of insight entered my brain and I realised why the mother was so eager to snatch the rope from me and with what kind of trade she was planning to console herself'.*

XXXI *Vocations*

In a beautiful garden, where the rays of the autumnal sun seemed to take pleasure in lingering, under a sky which had already turned a shade of green and in which golden clouds floated like travelling continents, four fine children,* four boys, no doubt tired of playing, were chatting together.

One said: 'Yesterday I was taken to the theatre. In great, gloomy palaces, at the back of which you can see the sea and the sky, men and women, who are serious and gloomy, too, but far more handsome and better dressed than those we see all about us, speak in lilting tones. They threaten each other, plead with each other, are filled with despair, and often they grasp a dagger thrust into their belt. Oh! its really beautiful! The women are really much lovelier and much taller than those who come and see us at home, and although their great hollow eyes and bright red cheeks make them look terrifying, you can't help loving them. You're frightened, you want to cry, and yet, you're happy ... And then, what's even stranger, it makes you want to dress the same, to say what they do and act as they do, and speak in a voice like theirs ...'

One of the four children, who for some seconds had stopped listening to what his friend was saying and had been staring with astonishing attention at a point in the sky, suddenly said: 'Look, look over there! Can you see *Him*? He's sitting on a little cloud all on its own, that little cloud that is the colour of fire, moving gently along. And what's more, *He* too seems to be looking at us.'

'But who do you mean?' asked the others.

'God!', he answered in tones of complete conviction. 'Oh!, he's already far away; soon you won't be able to see him any more. He's probably travelling, paying visits to all the countries of the world. There, he's just about to go behind that line of trees which is almost on the skyline ... and now he's going down behind the steeple ... Oh! you can't see him any more!' And for a long time the child remained looking in the same direction, staring at the line which separates earth and sky with eyes glowing with an ineffable expression of ecstasy and longing.

'What a booby he is, with his good Lord that he's the only one to see!' said at that point the third boy, whose entire little being was marked by an extraordinary liveliness and vitality. 'Now I'm going to tell you how something happened to me that has never happened to you and which is rather more interesting than your theatre and your clouds. — A few days ago, my parents took me on a journey with them and as there weren't enough beds for all of us in the inn where we stopped, it was decided that I would sleep in the same bed as my maid.' He drew his friends closer to him and lowered his voice. 'It's really odd, believe me, not to be in bed alone, but to be with your maid, in the dark. As I wasn't sleeping, I amused myself while she slept by running my hand over her arm, her neck, and her shoulders. Her arms and neck are much fatter than those of all the other women and the skin is so soft, so very soft that it seems like writing paper or paper made of silk. It was so nice that I'd have gone on doing it for a long time, if I hadn't been afraid, firstly of waking her up, and then of I don't know what. Then I burrowed my head in her hair as it hung down her back, as thick as a horse's mane, and it smelled as good, I can assure you, as flowers in the garden at this time of day. When you get a chance, try to do what I did and then you'll see!'*

As he told his story, the small author of this prodigious revelation stared with eyes stretched wide by a kind of stupefaction at what he still felt, and the rays of the setting sun, as they slipped through the russet curls of his disordered hair, illuminated it to form something like a sulphuric halo of passion. It was easy to guess that this one would not waste his life seeking Heaven in the clouds and that he would find it frequently elsewhere.

Finally, the fourth child said: 'You know it's no fun for me at home; I'm never taken to the theatre; my guardian is too stingy; God takes no notice of me and my boredom, and I don't have a beautiful maid to mollycoddle me. It's often struck me that I'd like to wander on forever without knowing where I was going and without anyone worrying about me, and that I'd like to see new countries all the time. I'm never content wherever I am, and I always feel I'd be better anywhere but where I happen to be. Well! At the last fair that was held in the neighbouring town, I saw three men who live as I'd like to live. You took no notice of them, you others. They were tall, almost black, and very proud, although they were in rags, and they looked as though they didn't need anyone. Their big dark eyes really gleamed when they played music, and that music was so surprising that sometimes it made you want to dance and sometimes it made you want to cry or to do both at the same time and you felt you'd go mad if you listened to it for too long. One, when he dragged his bow over his violin, seemed to be telling you his sorrows, the other, when his little hammer leapt along the strings of a small piano attached to his neck by a strap, seemed to be mocking his neighbour's complaint, while the third would clash his cymbals together from time to time with amazing violence. They were so pleased with themselves that they went on playing their wild music even after the crowd had dispersed. At last they picked up their coins, loaded their baggage on their backs, and set off. I wanted to know where they lived so I followed them from a distance right to the edge of the forest, and it was only there that I realized they didn't live anywhere.

Then one of them said: "Do we need to unpack the tent?" "Goodness no!", replied another, "it's such a lovely night!"

The third man said as he counted the takings: "Those folk don't appreciate music and their women dance like bears. Happily, in a month's time we'll be in Austria where we'll find people who are more congenial." "We might do better to go to Spain since the days are drawing in; let's flee from the rain and only get our throats wet!", said the other two.

I remember everything, as you see. Finally each of them drank a mug of brandy and fell asleep, their faces turned towards the stars. At first I wanted to beg them to take me with them and teach me to play their instruments; but I didn't dare, probably because it's always very hard to make a decision and also because I was afraid I'd be caught before we got out of France.'

The uninterested air of the other three friends made me think that this child was already *misunderstood*. I looked at him attentively. In his eye and on his brow there was some precociously fatal sign that generally alienates sympathy but which, I don't know why, aroused my own fellow feeling, to the extent that for a moment I had the bizarre impression that I might have a brother who was unknown to me.

The sun had set. The night in all its solemnity had taken its place. The children separated, each going, unaware. according to circumstance and chance, to ripen his fate, scandalize his friends, and gravitate towards glory or dishonour.

XXXII *The Thyrsus*

For Franz Liszt

What is a thyrsus?* In the moral and poetic sense of the word, it's a priestly emblem in the hands of those priests and priestesses celebrating the divinity of whom they are the servants and interpreters. But physically speaking it's only a stick, nothing but a stick. It can be a stake used for supporting hops or vines, something dry. hard, and straight. Around this stick, in capricious meanders, play and frolic stems and flowers, some like sinuous runaways, others leaning over like bells or upside-down cups. And an astonishing glory bursts from this complexity of lines and colours, tender and startling. Does it not seem that the curved line and the spiral pay court to the straight line and dance around it in silent adoration? Does it not seem that all these delicate corollas, all these calyxes, these explosions of perfume and colour, perform a mystical fandango around the hieratic stick? And yet who is the impudent mortal who would dare decide whether the flowers and the tendrils were made for the stick or whether the stick is merely a pretext to reveal the beauty of the tendrils and flowers? The thyrsus represents your astonishing duality, oh powerful and revered master, dear Bacchant of mysterious and passionate Beauty. Never has a nymph, goaded by unconquerable Bacchus, shaken her thyrsus over the heads of her maddened companions with as much energy and caprice as you employ when you shake your genius over the hearts of your brothers.—The stick is your will-power, straight, firm, and unmovable; the flowers represent your fantasy wandering around your will; they are the feminine element executing around the masculine element its prestigious pirouettes. Straight line and arabesque, intention and expression, firmness of the will, sinuosity of the word, unity of the aim, variety in the means, an all-powerful and indivisible amalgam of genius, what analyst would have the odious courage to divide and separate you?

Dear musician, through the mists, beyond the rivers, above the towns where pianos sing of your glory, and the printing presses translate your wisdom, wherever you may be, in the splendours of the eternal city or in the mists of the dreaming lands Cambrinus* consoles, improvising songs of delight or of ineffable grief, or entrusting to paper your abstruse meditations, singer of eternal Pleasure and unending Anguish, philosopher, poet, and artist, I salute you in immortality!

XXXIII *Never be Sober*

You must always be intoxicated. That sums it all up: it's the only question. In order not to feel the horrible burden of Time which breaks your back and bends you down to earth, you must be unremittingly intoxicated.

But on what? Wine, poetry, virtue, as you please. But never be sober.

And if it should chance that sometimes, on the steps of a palace, on the green grass of a ditch, in the bleak solitude of your room, you wake up and your intoxication has already diminished or disappeared, ask the wind, the wave, the star, the bird, the clock, ask everything that flees, everything that groans, everything that rolls, everything that sings, everything that speaks, ask them what time it is and the wind, the wave, the star, the bird, the clock, will reply: 'It's time to be intoxicated! If you do not wish to be one of the tortured slaves of Time, never be sober; never ever be sober! Use wine, poetry, or virtue, as you please.'

XXXIV *Already!*

A hundred times already the sun had leapt forth, radiant or sorrowful, from that immense bowl of the sea whose edges one can only just make out; a hundred times it had plunged back, sparkling or leaden, into its immense evening bath. For a number of days we had been able to contemplate the other side of the firmament and decipher the celestial alphabet of the antipodes. And each of the passengers grumbled and groaned. It seemed that the approach of land exasperated their suffering. 'When on earth', they would say, 'will we cease to sleep shaken by the billows, disturbed by a wind which snores more loudly than we do? When will we be able to eat meat which is not salted like the infamous element that carries us? When will we be able to digest our meals in a chair that keeps still?'

There were those who thought of their homes and missed their unfaithful and sulky wives, their screaming offspring. All were so maddened by the thought of the land they could not see that I believe they would have eaten grass with more enthusiasm than would animals.

At last landfall was sighted; and we saw as we approached that it was a magnificent land, a dazzling land. It seemed that life's music arose from it in a vague murmur and that from its shores, rich in all kinds of greenery, there wafted, for a distance of several leagues, a delicious odour of flowers and fruit.

Immediately everyone was joyous, everyone abandoned their bad moods. All quarrels were forgotten and all reciprocal ills were pardoned; duels which had been arranged were expunged from memory; and rancour drifted away like smoke.

I alone was sad, unimaginably sad. Like a priest whose divinity has been torn from him, I could not, without an overwhelming bitterness, detach myself from a sea so monstrously seductive, from that sea which has such infinite variety in its terrifying simplicity, and which seems to contain within itself and represent in its games, its movement, its anger and smiles, the moods, the agonies, and the ecstasies of all the souls that have lived, that are living, and that are yet to live!

In bidding farewell to this incomparable beauty, I felt myself crushed to the point of death, and that is why when each of my companions said: 'At last!', I could only cry; '*Already!*'

Yet it was the earth, the earth with its noises, its passions, its commodities, its festivals; it was a land which was rich and magnificent, full of promise, from which wafted a mysterious perfume of rose and musk, and from which the music of life reached us in an amorous murmur.

XXXV *The Windows*

Someone who looks in from the outside through an open window never sees as much as someone who looks through a closed window. There is no object more profound, more mysterious, more fertile, more shadowy, more dazzling than a window lit by a candle. What one can see in sunlight is always less interesting than what happens behind a pane of glass. In that dark or glowing hole life lives, dreams, suffers.

Beyond waves of roofs I can see a mature woman, already wrinkled, poor, constantly bending over something, a woman who never goes out. From her face, her clothes, her gestures, from almost nothing at all, I have reforged the life story of that woman, or rather her legend, and sometimes I recount it to myself, sobbing as I do.

Had it been a poor old man, I would have reforged his story just as easily.

And I go to bed, proud that I have lived and suffered in characters other than my own.

Perhaps you will say to me: 'Are you sure that that legend is the right one?' What does external reality matter, if it has helped me to live, to feel that I am and what I am?

XXXVI *The Desire to Paint*

Unhappy may be the man, but happy the artist pierced by passion!

I burn to paint the woman who appeared before me so rarely, and who fled so swiftly, like something beautiful and longed for that a traveller loses from view as he is whisked away into the night. How long it is already since she disappeared!

She is beautiful, she is more than beautiful; she is surprising. In her, black abounds; and everything she inspires is nocturnal and deep. Her eyes are two caverns faintly glittering with mystery, and her gaze illuminates like a flash of lightning; it is an explosion in the darkness.

I would compare her to a black sun, if one could conceive of a black star radiating light and happiness. But she makes one think more of the moon, which has surely marked her with its redoubtable influence; not the white moon of idylls, which resembles a cold bride, but the sinister and intoxicating moon, suspended in the depths of a stormy night and buffeted by the rushing clouds; not the peaceful, discreet moon dropping in on the sleep of the pure, but the moon wrenched from the sky, defeated and indignant, that the Thessalian sorceresses harshly oblige to dance on the terrified grass!*

Behind her low brow dwell tenacious will-power and the love of the prey. And yet, lower down this disquieting face, where the mobile nostrils inhale the unknown and the impossible, there explodes, with indescribable grace, the laughter of a wide mouth, red and white, and delicious, which prompts dreams of a miraculous and superb plant which has burst into flower in volcanic soil.

There are women who inspire the longing to defeat them and enjoy them; but the desire this woman awakens is that of dying slowly under her gaze.

XXXVII *The Benefits of the Moon*

The Moon, which is caprice itself, looked through the window while you slept in your cradle and said to herself: 'I like that child'.

And she slipped smoothly down her fleecy staircase of clouds and glided silently through the window panes. Then she lay upon you with a mother's supple tenderness and placed her own colours on your face. It's because of this that your eyes are green and your cheeks extraordinarily pale. It's in contemplating this visitor that your eyes grew so bizarrely wide, and she hugged your throat so tenderly that you have forever felt the desire to weep.

Nevertheless, in the expansion of her joy, the Moon filled

the whole room like a phosphorescent atmosphere, like a luminous poison; and all this living light thought and said: 'You will eternally feel the influence of my kisses. You will be beautiful in the way in which I am beautiful. You will love what I love and what loves me; water, clouds, silence, and night; the immense green sea; uniform and multiform water; those places where you are not; the lover you do not know; monstrous flowers; perfumes which drive you to delirium; cats swooning on pianos and moaning like women, with their rough, sweet voices!

And you shall be loved by those who love me, wooed by those who woo me. You shall be the queen of those green-eyed men whose throats I have also hugged in my nocturnal caresses; those who love the sea, the boundless sea, tumultuous and green, uniform and multiform water, the place where they are not, the woman they do not know, sinister flowers that resemble the incense containers of an unknown religion, perfumes that perturb the will, and the wild and voluptuous animals that are the emblems of their madness.'

And it is for that reason, my accursed and beloved spoilt child, that I now lie at your feet, seeking in all you are the reflection of that redoubtable Divinity, the fatal godmother, the poisoning wet-nurse of all *lunatics*.

XXXVIII *Which is the Real Benedicta?*

I knew a certain Benedicta, who filled the atmosphere with the ideal, and whose eyes radiated the desire for grandeur, beauty, glory, and all that makes us believe in immortality.

But that miraculous girl was too beautiful to live long; and therefore she died a few days after I had met her, and it was I myself who buried her on a day when spring was swinging its censer even in the cemeteries themselves. It was I who buried her, sealed tightly in a coffin made of a wood as perfumed and incorruptible as the chests of India.

And as my eyes were glued to the place where my treasure was buried, I suddenly saw a little person who bore a singular resemblance to the deceased, and who, stamping on the freshly dug ground with hysterical and bizarre violence, said as she burst into laughter: 'I'm the real Benedicta! It's me! one of the real riff-raff! And to punish you for your madness and your blindness, you will love me as I am!'

But I, in a fury replied: 'No! No! No!' And to give greater emphasis to my refusal, I stamped the earth so violently that my leg sank up to the knee in the freshly dug grave and, like a wolf caught in a trap, I remain attached, perhaps forever, to the grave of the ideal.

XXXIX A Thoroughbred Horse

She is really ugly. And yet she is delicious!

Time and Love have marked her with their talons and have cruelly taught her just how much youth and freshness are taken away by every minute that passes and every kiss that's exchanged.

She is truly ugly; she is an ant, she is a spider, if you will, even a skeleton; but she is also a drink, a potion, sorcery! in a word, exquisite.

Time has failed to undo the scintillating harmony of her stride or the indestructible elegance of her frame. Love has not altered the sweetness of her childlike breath; and Time has seized nothing of her abundant mane from which arises in wild perfumes all the turbulent vitality of the South of France, of Nîmes and Aix, Arles and Avignon, Narbonne and Toulouse, cities which are blessed by the sun, cities which are loving and charming!

Time and Love have truly gnawed away at her unabashed; they have done nothing to diminish the vague but eternal charm of her boyish chest.

Worn perhaps but not wearied, and always heroic, she makes one think of those truly thoroughbred horses which the eye of all true connoisseurs can recognize, even harnessed to a carriage for hire, or to a heavy cart.

And then, she is so gentle and so fervent! She loves as one loves in autumn; it seems that the approach of winter kindles

in her heart a fresh fire, and the servility of her tenderness
has nothing in it that is wearying.

XL *The Mirror*

A horribly ugly man comes in and looks at himself in the glass.

'Why do you look at yourself in the mirror, since you can't
see your reflection with anything but displeasure?'

The horribly ugly man replies: 'Sir, according to the immortal
principles of '89, all men have equal rights; therefore I possess
the right to look at myself in the mirror; whether pleasurably
or not concerns my conscience alone.'

From the point of view of good sense, I was undoubtedly
in the right; but, from the point of view of the law, he was
not in the wrong.

XLI *The Port*

A port is a charming sojourn for a soul weary of the struggles
of life. The vastness of the sky, the mobile architecture of the
clouds, the changing colours of the sea, the glittering of the
lighthouses, are a wonderfully appropriate prism for amusing
the eyes without ever tiring them. The slender shapes of the
ships, with their complicated rigging, which follow the har-
monious oscillations of the swell, serve to maintain in the mind
the taste for rhythm and beauty. And, then, above all, there
is a kind of mysterious and aristocratic pleasure for the man
who is no longer curious or ambitious, which consists in contem-
plating, as he lies in the belvedere or leans on the mole, all
the movements of those who set out and those who come back,
those who still have the strength to want anything, the desire
to travel or to grow rich.

XLII *Portraits of Mistresses*

In a male boudoir, by which I mean a smoking room attached
to an elegant dive, four men were smoking and drinking. You

couldn't really call them young, nor could you really call them old; they were neither handsome nor ugly; but old or young, they bore that unmistakable mark of old campaigners of pleasure, that indescribable something, that cold and scoffing sorrow that says clearly: 'We have lived intensely and we are seeking something we might love and value.'

One of them turned the conversation to the subject of women. It would have been more philosophical not to speak of them at all; but there are men of wit who, after drinking, do not despise banal conversations. In such circumstances you listen to the person speaking, just as you'd listen to dance music.

'All men,' the speaker was saying, 'have gone through the age of Cherubino:* this is the stage when, since you can't find any wood-nymphs, you feel no disgust at embracing the trunks of oak-trees. At the next stage, you begin to be more choosy. The ability to deliberate is already a form of decadence. It's at this stage that you really seek out beauty. As for me, gentlemen, I take credit in having long since reached the climacteric stage of the third degree where beauty itself is no longer sufficient, if it is not seasoned with perfume, finery, and so forth. I will even admit that I sometimes long, as one longs for an unknown happiness, for a certain fourth degree which must be that of absolute calm. But, throughout my entire life, apart from the Cherubino stage, I was more sensitive than anyone else to the enervating folly and the irritating mediocrity of women. What I love above all in those animals is their candour. So just imagine how much I had to suffer from my last mistress.

She was a prince's bastard. It goes without saying that she was beautiful; if she hadn't been, why would I have taken her? But she spoilt that great quality by unseemly and twisted ambition. She was a woman who always wanted to appear a man.* "You're not a man! Oh, if only I were a man! Of the two of us, I'm the one who's the man!" Such were the unbearable refrains which issued from a mouth from which I would have wanted to hear nothing but songs. If I revealed my admiration for a book, a poem, an opera: "You think, perhaps, that that's really great?", she would say immediately,

"What do you know about greatness?" and she would argue about it.

One fine day she took up chemistry; with the result that henceforth between my mouth and hers I always found a mask of glass. In addition to all that she was very prudish. If I sometimes jostled her with a gesture that was slightly too amorous, she would curl up as if she were a mimosa that had been attacked...'

'How did it end?', asked one of the other three. 'I wouldn't have thought you so patient.'

'God', he answered, 'provided the remedy with the disease. One day I found my Minerva, starved of idealized strength, in a tête-à-tête with my servant, and in a situation which forced me to retire discreetly to save their blushes. That night I dismissed the pair of them, paying them the wages due to them.'

'For my part,' said the one who had interrupted, 'I have only myself to blame. Happiness came to dwell with me and I did not recognize it. Fate in recent years granted me the pleasure of a woman who was the sweetest, most submissive and devoted of creatures, and always ready! and without any enthusiasm! "I'm perfectly willing, since it gives you pleasure." That was her usual reply. You could give the wall or the sofa a drubbing and you'd get more sighs from them than the wildest love drew from the breast of my mistress. After a year spent together she admitted to me that she had never experienced pleasure. I lost the taste of this unequal duel and that incomparable girl married someone else. I later took it into my head to see her again, and she said to me as she showed me her six lovely children: "Well, my dear, the wife is still just as much a *virgin* as your mistress was." Nothing had changed in her. Sometimes I miss her: I ought to have married her.'

The others burst out laughing, and a third took his turn to speak: 'Gentlemen, I have known pleasures that you may well have ignored. I mean the comic side of love, a comic side which does not exclude admiration. I admired my latest mistress more than you, I believe, hated or loved your own. And every-

one admired her just as much as I did. Whenever we went
into a restaurant, everyone, after a few minutes, would forget
to eat in order to gaze at her. The waiters themselves and
the woman dealing with the bills experienced this contagious
ecstasy to the point of forgetting their duties. In a word, I lived
for some time in the sole company of a living *monster*.* She ate,
chewed, crushed, devoured, swallowed, but did it all in the
lightest and most carefree manner in the world. In this way
she kept me long in ecstasy. She had a way of saying: "I'm
hungry" which was gentle, dreamy, English, and highly roman-
tic. And she would repeat those words night and day, revealing
the prettiest teeth in the world, teeth which would have both
moved and amused you. I could have made my fortune in
showing her at fairs as an *omnivorous monster*. I fed her well;
and yet she left me . . .'

'For a food merchant, no doubt?'

'Something of the sort, a kind of employee in the Supply
Corps, who through a wave of the wand he alone knew may
well have provided this poor child with the rations of several
soldiers. At least, that's what I supposed.'

'As for me', said the fourth, 'I endured atrocious suffering
through the very opposite of what we usually accuse in the
selfish female. I don't think you have the slightest grounds,
you over-fortunate mortals, for complaining about your mis-
tresses' imperfections!'

This was said in a very serious tone, by a man who appeared
gentle and self-controlled, with an almost clerical face, unfortu-
nately lit by two light-grey eyes, eyes whose gaze said: 'I want!',
or 'It must be!', or 'I never forgive!'

'If, you, G., as highly strung as I know you to be, or you
two, K. and I., as faint-hearted and fickle as I know you are,
if you had been coupled with a certain woman I knew, you
would either have taken to your heels or you would be dead.
As for me, I survived, as you see. Imagine someone incapable
of committing a single error either of sentiment or calculation;
imagine a distressing serenity of character; devotion free of
comedy or exaggeration; gentleness without weakness; energy
without violence. The story of my love resembles an endless

voyage on a surface as pure and polished as a mirror, dizzying in its monotony, which reflected all my feelings and my gestures with the ironic exactness of my own conscience, so that I could not allow myself a single unreasonable gesture or feeling without immediately seeing the unspoken reproach of my inseparable spectre. Love seemed to me to be a form of guardianship. How many stupid acts she stopped me performing, acts I regret not having committed! How many debts I paid in spite of myself! She deprived me of all the benefits I could have drawn from my personal madness. Her cold and inflexible rule put a stop to all my whims. The final straw in all this horror was that she never asked for thanks once the danger had passed. How many times did I stop myself leaping at her throat and screaming at her: "You wretch, be imperfect for a change! so that I can love you without feeling uneasy and angry!" For several years I admired her, my heart full of hate. But after all, I'm not the one that died of it.'

'Oh!', said the others, 'she's dead, then?'

'Yes, it couldn't go on like that. Love had become a crushing nightmare for me. Victory or death, as Politics says, that was the alternative that fate imposed upon me! One evening, in a wood ... beside a pool ... after a melancholy stroll in which her eyes had reflected the softness of the heavens and my heart was as fraught as Hades ...'

'What?'

'What are you saying?'

'What do you mean?'

'It was inescapable. I have too strong a sense of justice to beat, insult, or dismiss a servant who is beyond blame. But I had to find a balance between that feeling and the horror this creature inspired in me; I had to get rid of her without being disrespectful to her. What else would you have had me do with her, *given that she was perfect?*'

His three companions looked at him with a vague and somewhat stunned gaze, as if pretending not to understand and implicitly admitting that they themselves did not feel capable of so rigorous an action, although the reason for it was, nevertheless, sufficient.

Then they ordered fresh bottles, to kill Time which clings so tenaciously to life, and accelerate Life which passes so slowly.

XLIII *The Gallant Marksman**

As the carriage was going through the wood, he ordered it to stop in the neighbourhood of a firing range, saying that it would give him pleasure to shoot a few rounds in order to *kill* Time. Isn't killing that monster the most ordinary and legitimate occupation anyone can have? And he gallantly offered his hand to his beloved, his delicious and execrable wife, to that mysterious wife to whom he owes so many pleasures and so many sorrows, and perhaps, too a great part of his genius.

Several bullets landed wide of the chosen target; one of them even embedded itself in the ceiling; and as the charming creature was laughing madly, mocking her husband's clumsiness, he swung round to face her and said: 'You see that doll on the right over there, the one with her nose in the air and a stuck-up look on her face? Well, my angel, *I'm going to imagine it's you.*' And he closed his eyes and pulled the trigger. The doll was cleanly decapitated.

Then he bowed to his beloved, his delicious, his execrable wife, his unavoidable and unpitying Muse, and kissing her hand respectfully he added: 'Oh! my dear Angel! How much I thank you for my skill!'

XLIV *The Soup and the Clouds*

My mad little beloved was making dinner for me, and through the open window of the dining room I was contemplating the moving architecture that God creates with mists, the marvellous constructions of the impalpable. And I was saying to myself, in mid-contemplation: 'All that phantasmagoria is almost as beautiful as the eyes of my beautiful beloved, the monstrous little madwoman with her green eyes.'

And suddenly I received a violent punch in the back and heard a husky and charming voice, a hysterical voice, a voice made hoarse with brandy, the voice of my dear little beloved, which said: 'Are you going to hurry up and eat your soup, or aren't you, you b ... b ... of a cloud merchant?'

XLV *The Firing Range and the Cemetery*

—*The Inn Overlooking the Cemetery.* 'A curious inn sign', our stroller said to himself, 'but well chosen to make you thirsty! I bet the landlord appreciates Horace and the poets who follow the teaching of Epicurus. Perhaps he even knows the profound refinement of the Egyptians for whom no feast had any value if there were no skeleton present, or some emblem or other depicting the brevity of life.'

And he went in, drank a glass of beer overlooking the tombs, and slowly smoked a cigar. Then he had a fancy to go into the cemetery, where the grass was high and so inviting and where the sunlight held sway so richly.

In truth, light and heat raged there and it seemed that the drunken sun was wallowing full length on a carpet of magnificent flowers, fertilized by decay. A vast hum of life filled the air—the life of the infinitely small—interrupted at regular intervals by the rattle of gunshot from the next-door firing range, which exploded like the popping of champagne corks against the hum of a muted symphony.

Then, under the sun which warmed his brain and in the atmosphere of the blazing perfumes of Death, he heard a voice whispering from the tomb on which he was sitting. And that voice was saying: 'Cursed be your targets and your carbines, you, the turbulent living, who show so little concern for the dead and their divine repose! Cursed be your ambitions, cursed be your calculations, impatient mortals, you who come to study the art of killing beside the sanctuary of Death! If you knew how easy it is to win the prize, how easy it is to hit the target, how all, but Death, is nothingness, you would not weary yourselves so much, you, the laborious living, and you would disturb less often the sleep of those who have long since hit the target, the one true target of detestable life!'

XLVI *Loss of a Halo**

'Good gracious! You here, my dear? You, in a den of iniquity! You, the drinker of quintessences! You, the eater of ambrosia! Truly, it's enough to surprise me.'

'My dear, you know how terrified I am of horses and vehicles. A moment ago, as I was crossing the boulevard, in great haste, and hopping over the mud, through that moving chaos where death arrives at the gallop from all directions at once, my halo, in a sudden movement, slipped from my head and fell into the mire of the tarmac. I didn't have the courage to pick it up. I thought it would be less disagreeable to lose my insignia than to break my bones. And then, I said to myself, it's an ill wind that blows no one any good. Now I can stroll about incognito, perform despicable acts, indulge in the pleasures of the scum, like ordinary mortals. And here I am, just like you, as you see!'

'You should at least advertise the loss of your halo or ask the police to find it for you again.'

'Good Lord, no! I feel perfectly happy here. You're the only one who recognized me. Moreover dignity bores me. And what's more, it's a delight to think that some bad poet will pick it up and impudently stick it on his head. What pleasure it would give me to make someone happy! And especially if that someone also made me laugh! Just think of X or Z! Hey? Wouldn't it be funny!'

XLVII *Miss Scalpel*

As I came to the furthest reaches of the suburbs, under the gas lights, I felt an arm slip gently under mine and I heard a voice which whispered in my ear: 'Are you a doctor, sir?'

I looked; it was a tall girl, robust, her eyes very wide open, lightly made-up, her hair floating in the wind with the ribbons of her bonnet.

'No, ı m not a doctor. Let me go my ways.'

'Oh, yes, you're a doctor. I can see you are. Come home with me. I can give you a good time, I really can!'

'Of course I'll come and see you, but later, *after the doctor*, for heaven's sake! ...'

'Ha! Ha!, she said, still clinging to my arm, and bursting into laughter, 'You're a doctor who likes making jokes, I've known several of your sort! Come on.'

I am a passionate lover of mysteries because I continually hope to solve them. So I let myself be pulled along by this companion, or rather by this unlooked-for enigma.

I'll omit the description of the hovel; you can find it in several old and well-known French poets. Only, and this is a detail Régnier* didn't see, two or three portraits of famous doctors hung on the walls.

How I was spoilt! A blazing fire, a warm wine, cigars; and as she offered me these good things and lit up a cigar for herself, the funny creature said to me: 'Make yourself at home, my dear, make yourself comfortable. This will remind you of the hospital and the good days of your youth. Speaking of that, how did you get these white hairs? You weren't like that not long ago when you were one of L's interns. I remember it was you who assisted him in serious operations. Now *there's* a man who loves to cut and carve and trim! You were the one who used to hand him his instruments, his threads, and his sponges—And when the operation was over, he would say proudly as he looked at his watch: "Five minutes, gentlemen!"— Oh, I go everywhere. I know those gentlemen very well.'

A few instants later, addressing me informally, she was back on her hobby-horse again, and said to me: 'You are a doctor, aren't you, kitten?'

This meaningless refrain made me leap to my feet. 'No', I shouted, in a fury.

'A surgeon, then?'

'No, no! Except to cut your head off!' And I swore at her.

'Just a moment', she said, 'I'll show you something.'

She took out of a drawer a packet of papers, which consisted of nothing other than a collection of portraits of famous doctors of our day, lithographed by Maurin,* and which you used to see on display for several years on the quai Voltaire.

'Look, do you recognize this one?'

'Yes, that's X. Moreover, the name is written at the bottom; but I do know him personally.'

'I knew it! Look, there's Z, the one who described X to his students as: "That monster who wears on his face the blackness of his soul!" All that just because the other man was of a different opinion on a certain question! How they laughed about it at the Medical School at the time! You remember? Look, there's K, the one who denounced to the government the insurgents he was caring for in his hospital. That was at the time of the uprisings.* How can so handsome a man have so little heart? Now here's W, a famous English doctor; I caught him during his visit to Paris. He looks like a young lady, doesn't he?'

And as I picked up a packet tied with string which she'd also put on the table: 'Wait a moment', she said, 'those are the interns and this packet here is of the externs.'

And she spread out in the shape of a fan a mass of photographic images representing faces which were much younger.

'When we see each other again, you'll give me your portrait, won't you, darling?'

'But', I said, pursuing my own obsession, 'Why do you take me for a doctor?'

It's because you're so gentle and so kind to women!'

'Curious logic!', I said to myself.

'Oh, I rarely make a mistake; I've known a good number of them. I love those gentlemen so much that even though I'm not sick, I sometimes pay them a call, just to see them. There are some who say to me coldly: "You're not sick at all!" But there are others who understand me because I smile at them.'

'And when they don't understand you?'

Goodness me! As I've disturbed them *for nothing*, I leave ten francs on the mantelpiece—They're so good and so gentle, those men!—I discovered a little intern at the Hospital of Pity,

he's as pretty as an angel and so polite! And how he works,
the poor lad! His friends told me he hasn't a penny because
his family is poor and can send him nothing. That gave me
confidence. After all, I'm a pretty good-looking woman,
although I'm none too young. I said to him: "Come and see
me, come and see me often. And with me, you needn't worry;
I don't need any money." But you'll realize that I gave him
to understand this in a lot of different ways. I didn't just tell
him; I was so afraid I'd humiliate the dear child!—Well! Would
you believe there's something I'd really like that I daren't
mention to him? I'd love him to come and see me with his
instruments and his operating gown, even if there was a bit
of blood on it!'

And she said that with a very candid air, as a sensitive man
would say to an actress he loved: 'I want to see you wearing
the costume you wore in that famous role you created.'

But I, sticking to my guns, returned to the subject: 'Can
you remember the moment and the occasion when this special
passion was born in you?'

I had great difficulty making myself understood; finally I suc-
ceeded. But she replied with a very sad expression and even,
as far as I remember, turned her eyes away: 'I don't know
... I can't remember.'

What bizarre things we find in a big city, when we know
how to stroll about looking! Life swarms with innocent monsters.
Oh Lord, my God! You, the Creator, you, the Master; you
who made the Laws and who made Freedom; you the sovereign
who allows us to do as we will, you, the judge who forgives;
you who are full of reasons and causes, and who have perhaps
put into my mind a taste for horror in order to convert my
heart, as a cure at the tip of a blade; Lord, have pity, have
pity on the madmen and the madwomen! Oh Creator! Can
there exist monsters in the sight of Him who alone knows why
they exist, how they *made themselves*, and how they would have
been able *not to make themselves*?

XLVIII *Any Where Out of the World**

This life is a hospital in which each patient is possessed by the longing to occupy a different bed. While one longs to suffer close to the stove, another believes he would be healed if he could lie beside the window.

It seems to me that I would always be comfortable in the place where I am not, and the question of changing places is one I constantly debate with my soul.

'Tell me, my soul, my poor chilled soul, what would you say to living in Lisbon? It must be warm there and you would get your spirits back as if you were a lizard. The city lies beside the water; I'm told it's built of marble and that its people have such a hatred of the vegetable kingdom that they uproot all the trees. That would be a landscape in keeping with your tastes; a landscape of light and minerals, with the liquid element to reflect them!'

My soul makes no reply.

'Since you are so fond of repose, coupled with the spectacle of movement, would you like to live in Holland, that land that brings bliss? Perhaps you'll find amusement in that country whose image you have often admired in galleries. What would you say to Rotterdam, you who love forests of masts, and ships moored at the foot of houses?'

My soul keeps its silence.

'Batavia might attract you more, perhaps? There we would find, moreover, the spirit of Europe married to the beauty of the tropics.'

Not a word—could it be that my soul has died?

'Can you have grown so numb that you find pleasure only in what harms you? If that is the case, let us fly to those countries which offer analogies of Death—I know just what we need, poor soul! We will pack our bags for Torneo.* Let's go further still, to the furthest edge of the Baltic; still further from life, if that is possible; let us go and live at the Pole. There the sun's rays only touch the earth obliquely and the slow alternation of light and night suppresses variety and increases monotony, that other face of the void. There we can take long baths of darkness while, for our amusement, the Northern Lights send us from time to time their pink bouquets, like the reflections of a firework show in Hell!'

At last my soul erupts and shouts at me in its wisdom: 'Anywhere! Anywhere! as long as it's out of this world!'

XLIX *Let's Beat up the Poor!* *

For a fortnight I had confined myself to my room, and had surrounded myself with the sort of books that were in fashion in those days (this is some sixteen or seventeen years ago); I mean those books which deal with the art of making populations healthy, wealthy, and wise in twenty-four hours. I had therefore digested—swallowed, I should say—all the lucubrations of all those entrepreneurs of public happiness—those who advise all who are poor to become slaves, and those who persuade them that they are all kings whose thrones have been taken from them.—It will come as no surprise, therefore, that I was by that time in a state of mind bordering on dizziness or stupidity.

It merely seemed to me that I could feel, locked in the depths of my intellect, an obscure seed of an idea which was superior to the entire dictionary of old-wives' recipes I had just perused. But it was just the idea of an idea, something infinitely vague.

And I went out with a great thirst. For the impassioned taste for bad reading-matter engenders a proportional need for fresh air and refreshments.

As I was about to go into an inn, a beggar held out his cap with one of those unforgettable glances which would overturn thrones if mind could move matter, and if the eye of a hypnotist could ripen grapes.*

At the same moment I heard a voice whispering in my ear, a voice I easily recognized: it was the voice of a good Angel, or a good Demon, which accompanies me wherever I go. If Socrates had his good Demon, why should I not have my good Angel, and why would I not share with Socrates the honour of obtaining a certificate of madness, signed by the subtle Lélut and the most sensible Baillarger?*

Between Socrates's Demon and mine there is this difference,

that Socrates's Demon appeared before him only in order to forbid, warn, prevent, whereas mine deigns to advise, suggest persuade. Poor old Socrates only had a Demon who prohibited; mine is a great affirmer, mine is a Demon of action, a Demon of combat.

Well, this voice was whispering the following words to me: 'He alone is another man's equal who can prove himself to be so, and he alone is worthy of freedom who is able to seize it.'

Instantly I leapt on my beggar. With a single punch I closed one of his eyes, which in a second swelled up like a tennis ball. I broke one of my nails in knocking out two of his teeth and, as I didn't feel I was strong enough, being born delicate and having rarely practised boxing, to beat up this old man quickly, I seized the collar of his coat in one hand and with the other grasped his throat, and began to pound his head vigorously against a wall. I have to confess that I had first cast a glance around the area and had confirmed that in this deserted suburb I would for quite a long time be beyond the reach of any policeman.

Then, with a kick directed at his back, energetically enough to break his spine, I floored this enfeebled sexagenarian, and, seizing a large branch of a tree which was lying on the ground, I pounded him with the obstinate energy of cooks trying to soften a steak.

Suddenly—oh miracle! oh the joy a philosopher feels when he has confirmed the excellence of his theory!—I saw this antique carcass turn over, pick itself up with an energy I would never have suspected of a machine so singularly broken down, and with a glance of hatred which seemed to me an *excellent sign*, the decrepit brigand hurled himself at me, blacked both my eyes, broke four of my teeth, and with the self-same branch beat the living daylights out of me.—Through my energetic medication I had, therefore, restored to him both pride and life.

Then I made numerous signs to him to give him to understand that I considered the discussion closed, and getting up with the satisfaction of a sophist of the Portico,* I said to him: 'Sir, *you are my equal*! Pray do me the honour of sharing my purse with me; and remember, if you are a true philanthropist, that you should apply to all your confederates, when they request alms of you, the theory that I have had the *grief* of trying out on your back.'

He did indeed swear to me that he had fully understood my theory and that he would take my advice.

L *The Good Dogs*

For M. Joseph Stevens *

I have never blushed, even before the young writers of the age in which I live, at my admiration for Buffon; but today it is not the soul of this painter of Nature in all her pomp that I will summon to my aid. No.

I would far prefer to address myself to Sterne and I would say to him: 'Come down from the Heavens, or come up to me from the Elysian fields, to inspire me to write in favour of the good dogs, the poor dogs, a song worthy of you, sentimental prankster, incomparable prankster! Ride back astride that famous donkey who always accompanies you in the memory of posterity; and make sure above all that his donkey does not forget to carry, delicately hanging between his lips, his immortal macaroon!'*

Get thee behind me, Muse of the Academy! I have nothing to do with that old prude. I invoke the everyday Muse, the Muse of the city, the living Muse, so that she can help me sing of the good dogs, the poor dogs, the muddy dogs, those that everyone drives away, as if they were bearers of the plague and bearers of lice, all but the poor whose associates they are, and the poet who turns upon them the eye of a brother.

Fie on the classy dog, that four-footed fop, the Dane, the King Charles, the pug, or the spaniel, so enchanted with himself that he bounds indiscreetly against the legs or into the lap of the visitor, as if he were sure to please, as turbulent as a child, as stupid as a strumpet, sometimes as belligerent and insolent as a servant! Fie above all on those four-footed serpents, shivering and idle, that are called greyhounds and do not even have in their sharp muzzles enough sense of smell to follow the scent of a friend and whose flattened heads do not even contain enough intelligence to play dominoes!

Into your kennels, all you wearying parasites!

Send them back to their silky and padded kennels! I sing of the muddy dog, the poor dog, the homeless dog, the wandering dog, the acrobat dog, the dog whose instinct, like that of the poor, of gypsies, and of actors, is spurred on wonderfully by necessity, she who is so good a mother, she who is the true patroness of intelligence!

I sing of calamitous dogs, those who wander, all alone, in the sinuous ravines of immense cities, or those who have said to the abandoned man, with winking, witty eyes: 'Take me with you and with our two misfortunes we may perhaps make a kind of happiness!'

'*Where do the dogs go to?*', Nestor Roqueplan* once asked in an immortal article which he has doubtless forgotten, and which I alone, and perhaps Sainte-Beuve,* still remember today.

Where do the dogs go to, you ask, oh inattentive men! They go about their business.

Business meetings, love meetings. Through the fog, through the snow, through the mud, under the biting sun of the dog-days, under the streaming rain, they come, they go, they trot, they pass beneath vehicles, aroused by fleas, passion, need, or duty. Like us, they rose early, and they are gaining a livelihood or running in search of pleasures.

There are some who sleep in a ruin in the suburbs, and who come, each day, at the same hour, to demand the manna on offer at the kitchen door of the Palais-Royal; others who flock together from more than five leagues away to share the meal prepared for them by the charity of certain sexagenarian spinsters whose unoccupied hearts have turned to animals because men in their imbecility no longer want them.

Others who, like runaway slaves, maddened with love, leave their own areas, on certain days, to come into the city, gambol for an hour or so around a beautiful bitch, somewhat unkempt in her toilette but proud and grateful.

All are very punctual, although they have neither diaries nor notebooks nor wallets.

Do you know Belgium, that loafer, and have you admired, as I have, all the vigorous dogs harnessed to the butcher's cart, the milkmaid's cart, the baker's cart, dogs whose triumphant barking bears witness to the proud pleasure they experience in rivalling horses?

Here are two who belong to a still more civilized order. Allow me to bring you into the room of the absent entertainer. A bed, in painted wood, without curtains, covers trailing on the floor and stained by bedbugs, two straw chairs, a cast-iron stove, one or two broken musical instruments. Oh! how miserable the furniture is! But look, I beg you, at those two intelligent beings, dressed in clothes which are at once threadbare and sumptuous, wearing hairstyles reminiscent of troubadours or soldiers, who are as attentive as witches as they watch over the *work without a name**** that bubbles on the lit stove, and in the centre of which stands a long spoon, planted like one of those lofty masts which announce the completion of a building.

It is not fitting that such zealous actors should not set out without having ballasted their bellies with some powerful and solid soup? And could you not forgive a little sensuality in these poor devils who every day are obliged to confront the indifference of the public and the injustice of a director who takes the largest share and on his own eats more soup than four actors?

How often have I contemplated, smiling and moved, all those four-footed philosophers, those slaves, who are understanding, submissive, or devoted, which the republican dictionary could perfectly well qualify as *unofficial* slaves if the republic, too concerned with the *happiness* of man, had the time to deal tactfully with the *honour* of dogs!

And how often have I thought that somewhere or other there was perhaps (after all, who can tell?) as recompense for so much courage, so much patience, so much hard work, a special paradise for the good dogs, the poor dogs, the muddy and desolate dogs. Swedenborg affirms that there is indeed one paradise for Turks and another for the Dutch!

The shepherds of Virgil and Theocritus expected, in return for their alternating songs, a good cheese, a flute made by the best flute maker, or a goat with swollen udder. The poet who has sung of the poor dogs received in recompense a fine waist-coat, of a colour at once rich and faded, which evokes thoughts of autumn, of the beauty of mature women, and of Indian summers.

None of those who were present in the inn of Villa Hermosa street will ever forget the vitality with which the painter stripped off his waistcoat in favour of the poet, so well did he understand how good and honest it was to sing of the poor dogs.

Just as a magnificent Italian tyrant, of the good old days, offered to divine Aretino* either a dagger enriched with precious stones or a court mantle in exchange for a precious sonnet or a curious satirical poem.

And every time the poet dons the painter's waistcoat, he is obliged to think of the good dogs, the philosophical dogs, of Indian summers and the beauty of very mature women.

APPENDIX

*Plans and Projects**

Projected Dedication

The Gifts of the Fairies
The Cake

to Houssaye:
The Title
The dedication
[To Cat *crossed out*]
Without head or tail. All head and tail.
Handy for me. Handy for you. Handy for the Reader. We can all cut wherever we wish, I my reverie, you the manuscript, the reader his reading. And I do not tie the recalcitrant will to the unending thread of a superfluous plot.

I have searched for titles. The 66. Although, however, as this work resembles a screw or a kaleidoscope [it could be *crossed out*] it could easily be pushed as far as the cabalistic 666 or even 6666 . . .

[People should be grateful to me that *crossed out*]

[That's worth *crossed out*] That's worth more than a plot of 6000 pages. People should be grateful to me for my moderation.

Who among us has not dreamt of a particular prose, a poetic prose which could translate the lyrical movements of the mind, the undulations of reverie, the leaps of conscience?

My point of departure was Aloysius Bertrand. What he had done for the picturesque life of the past, I wanted to do for our modern, abstract life. And then, from the beginning, [I realized *added*] that I was doing something different from what I had sought to imitate. Something that for another would be a source of pride, but which humiliates me, for *I* believe that the poet must always do exactly what he sought to do.

Note on the famous expression.
Finally, little sections
the whole snake.

To Catrin*
The signature
The rest to follow shortly.

Projects

Poems to write

PARISIAN TOPICS

1.   The little old atheist
2.   The courtyard of the post office
3.   An Elegy to hats
4.   The black hen
5.   The End of the World
6.   From the heights of the Buttes Chaumont*
7.   One Ash Wednesday
8.   The Poet and the Historian
9.   Orestes and Pylades*
10.   The Two Drunkards
11.   The Mental Specialists
12.   The Philosopher at the carnival
13.   The Portrait's Reproaches
14.   The Gold Fish
15.   Flight of Riders
16.   Songs of the Church
17.   In Honour of my Patron Saint (4 November)
18.   Moloch's altar*
19.   For five sous
20.   The Seductive Undertaker
21.   The Room of Martyrs
22.   The Diamond Man
23.   The Old Lover
24.   Before Ripening
25.   The Barrel Organ
26.   The Deaf and Dumb Man
27.   The Distribution of Victuals
      A Parisian Lazzaronne* [*sic*]
28.   Hell at the Theatre
29.   The Gentle Visitor

30. Cholera at the Opera
31. Melancholia
32. The Inn in the Thicket
33. Wedding Nights
34. The Self-Cuckold or The Incestuous Man

DREAM WORLDS

35. Symptoms of ruin
36. My Beginnings
37. Return to College
38. Unknown Apartments
39. Landscapes without Trees
40. Condemnation to Death
41. Death
42. The Mouse Trap
43. Fiesta in a Deserted Town
44. The Palace on the Sea
45. The Staircases
46. Prisoner in a Lighthouse
47. A Desire

SYMBOLS AND MORALITIES

48. Filial Ingratitude
49. A Phrase of Jean Hus* [*sic*]
50. The Holy Illusion
[51. *crossed out*] Neither Remorse Nor Regrets
51. The Rococo Sphinx
52. The Great Prayer
53. Lucan's Last Songs
54. The Pharisee's Prayer.
      The Chapelet
      Let us not offend the Shades

Prose Poems

to do

48.² Let us not offend the Shades

77. A sudden change of wind direction

78. A rancour satisfied (a story of Feuchères (*sic*)* *perhaps a short story*)

79. The expectant father (madman's clothes, and toys, *perhaps a short story*)

80. # The Lazzaronne [*sic*] (In Paris)

81. # In Honour of my Patron Saint. (The Billiard Table)

82. Filial ingratitude (the birds) (experiment)

83. The warning dream (*perhaps a short story*)

84. The Inn in the Thicket (memory of youth, through the smell, the colour, the fresh wind)

85. # The poet and the historian (Carlyle and Tennyson)

86. # Symptoms of ruins

87. # My Beginnings

88. # Return to College (consultation)

89. # Unknown apartments. (Places known and unknown, but recognized. Dusty apartments. Moves. Books rediscovered.)

90. The palace on the sea

91. Landscapes without trees

92. The Mouse Trap

93. The Stairways. (Vertigo. Great Curves. Men hooked, a sphere, fog above and below.)

94. Prisoner in a lighthouse

95. Condemnation to death. (Fault I'd forgotten but suddenly recalled, since being condemned.)

96. Death

97. # The sacred illusion

98. Melencholia [*sic*]

99. # A desire

100. The Dream of Socrates

101. # A saying of Jean Hus [*sic*]

102. Neither remorse nor regrets(?)

103. Lucan's last songs

104. The rococo Sphinx

105. The Gentle Visitor

CATEGORIES

Parisian things

Dreams

Symbols and Moral Fables

Find other categories

106. # Cholera at the masked ball

107.   [The great prayer *crossed out*]
         Statistics and the Theatre
         (Hell in the theatre)

[108.   Everywhere, out of the world
         Any

109.   The Great Prayer] [*crossed out*]

110.   Let's Beat up the Poor (done)

111.   The Good Dogs (done)

112.   The Pharisee's Prayer

[Plans and Notes]

[A]   PROSE POEMS

Jean Hus [*sic*]. (analysis of his last words.)
The tall melancholy widow in front of Musard's garden.*
The poor people in front of a new café.
My dreams.

> Comedy in the provinces.
> The college.
> Death.
> The void. (Feeling of infinite emptiness.)
> Condemnation to death for a forgotten fault. (Feeling of fear. I do not dispute the accusation. A great fault which is not explained in my dream.)
> Unknown apartments, poor but noble and poetic.

The Old Mountebank.
The elegy on the hats. Flowers in the desert. The lines of Thomas Gray.*

[B]   PROSE POEMS

(For Civil War)
The cannon thunders ... limbs fly ... one can hear the groans of victims and howling from those performing the sacrifice ... It's Humanity seeking happiness.

[C]   NOCTURNAL POEMS

THE LETTER OF A FOOL.
A mixture of sincere exaggeration and ironic exaggeration.

There are days when I feel so powerful that . . .
The Mappa mundi.

[D]

Symptoms of ruin. Vast buildings. Several, one on top of the other, apartments, rooms, *some temples*, galleries, stairways, caeca, viewpoints, lanterns, fountains, statues.—*Fissures and cracks. Dampness resulting from a reservoir situated near the sky.*—How to warn people and nations? let us whisper warnings into the ears of the most intelligent.

High up, a column cracks and its two ends are displaced. Nothing has collapsed as yet. I can no longer find the way out. I go down, then climb back up. *A labyrinth-tower. I never succeeded in leaving. I live forever in a building on the point of collapsing, a building undermined by a secret malady.*—I work out in my mind, to amuse myself, if such a prodigious mass of stones, marbles, statues, walls, which are about to collide with each other, will be greatly sullied by that multitude of brains, human flesh, and shattered bones.—I see such terrible things in my dreams that sometimes I wish I could sleep no more, if I could be sure not to be too weary.

[E]   Notes for *The Elegy on Hats*
        A hat. Smooth surface.
        A cap. Folded or bubbling surface.
        The pass (from the spot which no longer sits on the head.)
        The part at the back is called the crown or dome, or the lining, when it is fluted.
        Bonnet strings. Fasteners or little ribbons.
        Feathers, marabous or aigrettes.
        Head bands, of feathers or flowers
        A *maintenon*, a kind of lace snood, fitted onto the hat and tied on above the ribbons.
        A *Mary Stuart*, a form in which the peak is very low, a Sarrasin or ogival shape.
        A *Lavallière* (gone out of fashion) with two feathers meeting behind.
        Russian hat. An aigrette.
        The little toque has a pompon or a wing.
        A flower (rose) placed on a *Marie-Louise*.
        A *Marinière* hat, with a bouquet.
        A *Longueville* hat is a Lavallière with a single feather which floats and flaps in the wind.

A Scottish hat, in poplin with squares, has a rosette, a silver clasp, and an eagle's or a raven's feather.

Ornaments: puffs, ruffs, bias cuts, borders.

The furnishing of a fashion shop:

Curtains in muslin or silk of a uniform white colour. Divans. Looking glass, a smooth, mobile surface. Oval, inclined mirrors. Large oval table, with a long-legged hatstand. A fairies' laboratory. A clean task.

General appearance: coolness, light, whiteness, the sparkling colours of a flower-bed.

Ribbons, frills, tulle, gauze, muslin, feathers, etc ...

The hats inspire thoughts of faces, and look like a gallery of faces. For each hat, because of its character, evokes a face and lets the mind's eye see it. Guillotined heads.

What sadness there is in this solitary frivolity! A distressing feeling of foolish ruin. A monument to gaiety standing in a desert. Frivolity in abandon.

The suburban milliner, pale, anaemic, milk coffee, like an old tobacconist.

A distressing feeling.

[F] *The Courtyard of the Post-Office*

In the middle of a group of various people getting down from a stage-coach, a woman surrounded by her children, throws herself into the arms of a traveller wearing a cotton bonnet. A cold Paris day. A child stands on tip-toes, to be kissed.

Further off, another traveller loads his parcels onto a delivery boy's pack.

In the foreground, on the left, a beggar holds out his hat to a soldier with a yellow plume, a mercenary, thin as Bonaparte, and a member of the national guard tries to embrace a succulent flower-seller carrying a basket; she defends herself half-heartedly.

On the right, a gentleman, hat in hand, talks to a woman carrying a child; near this group, two dogs are fighting. Boilly.* 1803.

[G]

Der Tod als Erwürger.*

Erster Auftritt des Cholera auf einem Maskenball in Paris, 1831.

Der Tod als Freund.

Death as executioner.

First appearance of cholera at a masked ball in Paris, 1831.

Death as friend.

SELECTION OF VARIANTS

'Le Crépuscule du soir'. After the first publication of this prose poem, in the *Hommage à Denecourt*, Baudelaire introduced substantial changes for a proposed publication in *La Presse* which did not eventuate. The text of the Denecourt volume was as follows:

Nightfall has always been for me the signal of an inner celebration and a form of deliverance from anguish. In the forests, as in the streets of a large city, the darkening of day and the glittering of stars or lanterns illuminates my mind.

But I had two friends whom dusk made ill. One would then be incapable of recognizing all bonds of friendship or politeness, and would savagely attack the first person he came across. I have seen him throw an excellent chicken at a head waiter. The coming of evening spoilt the best things for him.

The other as day fell became increasingly bitter, sombre, teasing. Indulgent during the hours of daylight, he was pitiless in the evening. And it was not only towards others but towards himself as well that his evening madness wreaked such abundant havoc.

The first died insane, unable to recognize his mistress and his child; the second carries within him the disquiet of perpetual dissatisfaction. The shadow which sheds light in my mind casts darkness in theirs.—And although it is not rare to see the same cause engender two contradictory effects, I am always intrigued and astonished when it does so.

'Solitude'. Again, after the initial publication in the Denecourt volume, Baudelaire considerably revised his poem for a planned publication in *La Presse* which did not eventuate. The first published version of the poem was as follows:

He also used to say to me—the second of these men—that solitude was bad for man, and he would quote, I think, the writings of the Church Fathers. It is true that the spirit of murder and lewdness is wonderfully inflamed in lonely places; the Devil often visits arid spots.

But that seductive solitude is dangerous only for idle and rambling souls who are not ruled by an important, active thought. Solitude was not bad for Robinson Crusoe; it made him religious, brave, industrious; it purified him, and taught him just how far an individual's strength can go.

Isn't it La Bruyère who talked about 'the great misfortune of not being able to be alone ...'? Loneliness, therefore, is like dusk; good and bad, criminal or salutary, incendiary or calming, according to the person concerned and how that person has lived.

As for pleasure—the most splendid brotherly feasts, the most magnificent meetings of men electrified by a pleasure shared with one another, will never give comparable pleasures to those experienced by the Solitary Man, who with a glance has embraced and understood all the sublimity of a landscape. That glance has acquired for him a property of his own which can never be taken from him.

'The Plans'. As for the previous two poems, the first version was greatly altered for a projected publication in *La Presse*. The text that appeared in *Le Présent* in 1857 is as follows:

How beautiful you would be in a complex and ornate gown for the court, descending, through the mists of a fine evening, the marble steps of a palace, opposite sweeping lawns and ornamental ponds!

But what need have we of such fine surroundings? How mad I am! I was forgetting how I hate roses and their palaces.—No, it is not in a palace that I'd like to possess you and enjoy your friendship. We wouldn't be *at home* there. Moreover, those walls that are as embossed, braided, insolent, and gleaming as soldiers resemble the Great King's soul and have no nooks allowing intimacy.—No *dreameries* [*rêvoirs*] here; on those walls which are covered with gold I can't see the slightest space for a nail from which to hang your picture.

Oh! I know where I'd really like to love you for ever and ever!—Beside the sea, a beautiful wooden hut, wrapped in shade! In the air would float an odour of coconut oil, and everywhere there would be an indescribable perfume of musk; on the horizon, tips of masts, which, through an indetectable movement of the swell, trace curves in the air. Around us, outside the dark, silent room full of flowers and mats, with its few pieces of furniture in Portuguese rococo style made from local wood, where you would rest so gently, so nonchalantly, so carefully fanned, smoking tobacco mixed with opium and sugar—beyond the verandah, the clamour of birds and the delicate chattering of negro women.

But no!—What is the point of such an enormous set?—It would cost a lot of money, and money dances only in the pockets of imbeciles who have no understanding of Beauty.—Pleasure is a few leagues from here, two steps away, in the first inn we come across, in a chance inn, so rich in happiness. A great fire, bright crockery on the walls, a bearable supper, a lot of wine, and a very wide bed with sheets which are a bit rough, but clean.

... Dreams, dreams, always those accursed dreams!—they kill action and eat time!—Dreams calm momentarily the ravening beast bounding within us. They are a poison which calms the beast but which also nourishes it.

Where then can one find a cup deep enough and a dagger thick enough to drown the *Beast*!

'The Rope'. The version published in *L'Artiste* on 1 November 1864 contained an additional, explanatory sentence at the end:

'Of course!', I answered my friend, 'A metre of the rope that a man has used to hang himself, at 100 francs for every ten centimetres, all in all, with everyone paying as best they can, that makes a thousand francs, and that's a real and effective relief for that poor mother!'

EXPLANATORY NOTES

2. *Plotinus*: third-century mystic.

   Porphyrius: third-century philosopher, disciple of Plotinus.

   Crébillon the younger: Claude-Prosper Jolyot de Crébillon (1707–77), French writer whose novels were frequently licentious.

   Cardano: Italian mathematician, doctor, philosopher (1501–76).

3. *Swedenborg*: Emanuel Swedenborg (1688–1772), Swedish theosopher.

4. *Mariette*: the name of Baudelaire's nursemaid when he was a child.

5. *Scott*: the novelist was extremely popular in France in the 1820s and 1830s, and greatly admired by Balzac and Hugo.

6. *Oudinot petticoat*: this was worn under an open or transparent dress. Oudinot was a highly fashionable designer at the time Baudelaire was writing.

7. *... hair so long*: parody of a traditional proverb according to which woman is an animal long on hair and short on ideas.

12. *Berquin*: Arnaud Berquin (1749–91), writer of moralistic and often very dull children's books. In an article, Baudelaire mentions thankfully that he was never obliged to read Berquin as a child.

16. *Tartuffe*: character in Molière's play of the same name, now synonymous with hypocrisy.

    Diderot: Denis Diderot (1713–84), French philosopher and writer.

17. *Valmont*: character from Laclos's *Dangerous Liaisons*. Epitomizes the kind of man who sees sexual relations merely in terms of power.

    Lovelace: character from Richardson's *Clarissa*: epitomizes the roué.

    Elmire: heroine of Molière's *Tartuffe*.

18. *Andalouseries*: poems in the manner of the Andalusian poets. This may be an allusion to Musset's *Tales of Spain and Italy*.

21. *Devéria*: Achille Devéria (1800–57), French painter, lithographer, and engraver. Best known for his illustrations of Romantic novels.

22. *Columbine, Marguerite, Elvire, and Zéphyrine*: Columbine is the her-
oine of the Commedia dell'arte plays; Marguerite is the heroine
of Goethe's *Faust*; Elvire is one of the women abandoned by
Don Juan in Molière's play and Mozart's opera; Zéphyrine is
one of the main characters in the well-known 'parade' *Les Saltim-
banques* by Domerson and Varin (1831). Baudelaire mentions the
hero of this piece in 1846 (see C. Pichois's note in Baudelaire's
Œuvres Complètes, ii: 1335). I am grateful to Dr G. Robb for the
information concerning Zéphyrine.

23. *Chattertons and Savages*: Thomas Chatterton (1752–70) and
Richard Savage (d.1743) typify the ill-starred poet.

24. *Paracelsus*: pseudonym of Theophrastus Bombast von Hohen-
heim (?1493–1541), Swiss alchemist, father of hermetic medicine.

29. *Auri sacra fames*: 'the terrible thirst for gold'. Virgil, *Aeneid* iii.
57.

   Nisard: Napoléon Désiré Nisard (1806–88), journalist and critic,
an ardent adversary of the Romantics.

30. *Houssaye*: Arsène Houssaye (1814–96), literary editor of *L'Artiste*
and editor of *La Presse*, also published a volume of poetry.

   Gaspard de la nuit: this collection of prose poems was published
posthumously in 1842. Bertrand (1807–41) drew inspiration for
his prose poems from medieval Dijon and created a prose form
which is reminiscent of the ballad in its structure.

   the Glazier: Houssaye's poem, published in *Poésies complètes* in 1850,
is flat, sentimental, and far more prosaic than poetic.

32. *The Old Woman's Despair*: Baudelaire's compassionate interest in
old women is reflected in several of his verse as well as his
prose poems. As early as 1851 he jotted down the following note
in Mme Francine Ledoux's *Liber amicorum*: 'What means can
I effectively use to convince a young feather-head that the irre-
sistible sympathy I feel for old women, those creatures who
have greatly suffered at the hands of their lovers, their husbands,
their children, and also through their own failings, contains
not a jot of sexual appetite?'

33. *the sense of self soon fades*: there are several parallel passages in
Baudelaire's writing. One might compare the following evoca-
tion from his 'Poem of Hashish': 'It sometimes happens that
the personality disappears completely and that objectivity, which
is the characteristic of pantheist poets, develops within you so

abnormally that the contemplation of external objects makes you forget your own existence, and soon you merge with them completely. Your eye fixes on a tree bent over by the wind; in a few seconds what, in the mind of a poet, would merely be a most natural comparison becomes for you a reality. First, you attribute your own passions to the tree, giving it your desires or your feeling of melancholy. Its groans and oscillations become your own, and soon you yourself are the tree. In the same way, the bird floating high up in the azure sky begins by *representing* the immortal desire to float above the things of this earth, but already you yourself have become the bird.'

35. *René*: Chateaubriand refers to the idealized woman of his youth in *René*, where she is not named, and in his *Mémoires d'outre-tombe* (*Memories from Beyond the Grave*), where he calls her Sylphide.

36. *To Each His Monster*: it is generally accepted that this poem was inspired by Goya's engraving entitled *Tu que no peudes* which depicts men staggering under the weight of donkeys. Goya's meaning is political, evoking the way in which Spain was being crushed by the fools in government: Baudelaire, typically, widens the metaphor to give it metaphysical dimensions.

39. *Minos, Aeacus, or Rhadamanthus*: judges of the Underworld.

41. *The tyranny of the human face*: Baudelaire borrows this expression from Thomas de Quincey, whose *Confessions of an English Opium Eater* he had adapted and translated.

  Venustre: she means, of course, Venus.

42. *a woman*: the wild woman was a frequent attraction at fairs in the nineteenth century.

43. *seize you, munch you, and kill you at its pleasure*: the reference is to La Fontaine's poem 'The Frogs who asked for a King', *Fables*, III, 4. Baudelaire transforms the quotation slightly.

45. *Vauvenargues*: Luc de Clapiers, Marquis de Vauvenargues (1715–47), French moralist. The statement referred to appears in his 'Reflections on diverse topics'.

  those whom life has maimed: one thinks here of Mme de Cosmelly.

51. *Which was true*: this anecdote was taken from Father Huc's famous study *The Chinese Empire*, which first appeared in 1854.

52. *Féline*: it is not certain who this is, although a copy of the second edition of *The Flowers of Evil* is dedicated to 'my very dear Féline'.

54. *Invitation to the Waltz*: the reference is to Carl Maria von Weber (1786–1826).

   black tulip ... blue dahlia: the fascination of the Dutch with such possibilities is reflected in Alexandre Dumas's novel *The Black Tulip* (1850) and a song by Pierre Dupont, whose work Baudelaire twice reviewed.

59. *Plutus*: the god of riches.

64. *Santerre*: Antoine Joseph Santerre (1752–1809). Given the mission of escorting Louis XVI to the guillotine, Santerre commanded his drummers to interrupt the king's farewell speech.

   La Bruyère: Jean de la Bruyère (1645–96), French moralist. The aphorism in question here occurs in a section called 'De l'homme' ('On Man'), in his famous work *Les Caractères*: 'all our evils befall us because we cannot be alone: this is what causes gambling, lechery, dissipation, wine, women, ignorance, slander, envy, and what makes us forget ourselves and God.' Poe quotes this in his short story 'Metzengerstein'.

   Pascal: Blaise Pascal (1623–62), philosopher, mathematician, and writer. This statement comes from the section called 'Divertissements' of his *Pensées* and proclaims: 'all the unhappiness of man comes from a single cause which is the inability to sit quietly in one's room'.

69. *Fancioulle*: this name may have a special meaning, since in Italian *fanciullo* means 'child'. For Baudelaire, genius was 'childhood rediscovered at will'.

75. *... soaring breakers*: R. Kopp has shown, in his edition of the prose poems, how much this passage owes to Tennyson.

76. *... former resentment*: this description is reminiscent of Mephistopheles' statement at the end of the Prologue in *Faust*:

> I like to see the Old Man now and then
> And try to be not too uncivil.
> It's charming in a noble squire when
> He speaks humanely with the very Devil.

   Tr. Walter Kaufmann (New York: Anchor Books, 1962). Baudelaire's friend Nerval published his translation of the play in 1840.

77. *Manet*: Baudelaire and the painter were on close terms. It has been established that the young model who posed for Manet's

Child with Cherries, Alexandre, did indeed hang himself in the artist's studio.

80. *... to console herself*: it was considered lucky to possess a piece of rope from which someone had hanged himself. The mother, therefore, plans to sell sections of the rope with which her son had committed suicide.

81. *children*: the importance Baudelaire placed on the influence of childhood for the adult's development should not be underestimated. In a passage he added to his adaptation of De Quincey's *Confessions of an English Opium Eater* he made the following assertion: 'the slightest sorrow or the slightest joy in childhood, inordinately magnified by an exquisite sensitivity, become in the adult, unbeknown to them, the basis of a work of art. . . . Would it not be easy to prove, through a philosophical comparison between the works of a mature artist and his state of mind in childhood, that genius is merely childhood clearly formulated and endowed with virile and powerful organs of expression?' He insists, moreover, in a study on Poe that 'the character, the genius, and the style of a man are formed by the apparently vulgar circumstances of his earliest youth. If all those who have occupied the world's stage had noted down their childhood impressions, what a marvellous psychological dictionary we would possess!'

82. *... you'll see*: in a letter of 23 April 1860 Baudelaire asserted to Poulet-Malassis, his editor, that any intelligent reader could perceive the sensuality of the child: 'what is it that the child loves so passionately in its mother, its nurse, its older sister? Is it simply the being who nourishes it, combs its hair, washes it, and rocks it? It is also the caress and the sensual pleasure she provides. For the child, this caress expresses itself, unbeknown to the woman, through all her grace. So the child loves its mother, its sister, its nurse because of the agreeable tickling of her satin and her furs, for the perfume of her breast and her hair, for the clicking of her jewellery, the play of her ribbons, etc., for all the *mundus muliebris* beginning with the blouse and expressing itself even through the furniture on which the woman has placed the imprint of her sex.'

84. *thyrsus*: Baudelaire himself comments on this word in the conclusion of his adaptation of De Quincey: '[De Quincey's thought] is the *thyrsus* of which he has so jokingly spoken, with the candour

of a vagabond who knows himself well. The subject has no value other than that of a dry, bare stick; but the ribbons, the vines, and the flowers can, through their mad intermingling, provide a precious richness for the eyes. De Quincey's thought is not only sinuous; the word is not strong enough; it is naturally spiral.'

85. *Cambrinus*: mythical character associated with the invention of beer.

88. *dance on the terrified grass*: the reference is to Lucan (AD39–65), *Pharsalia*, book VI, lines 499–506. Baudelaire frequently praised this work, defending Lucan against the contemporary critics Villemain and Janin.

92. *Cherubino*: character in Beaumarchais's play *The Marriage of Figaro*, who symbolizes the adolescent first awakening to love.

wanted to appear a man: here one might compare Baudelaire's comment on the Marquise de Merteuil in Laclos's *Dangerous Liaisons*: 'the woman who always wants to appear a man, sign that she is greatly depraved.'

94. *monster*: the word here has the specific meaning of an extraordinary person or thing put on show at fairs.

96. *The Gallant Marksman*: in his *Intimate Diaries* Baudelaire jotted down a first draft of this poem: 'A man goes to a firing range, acompanied by his wife.—He aims at the doll and says to his wife: "I'm imagining that doll is you."—He closes his eyes and hits the doll.—Then he says as he kisses his wife's hand: "Dear Angel, how I thank you for my skill!"'

98. *Loss of a Halo*: the first draft of this poem can be found in Baudelaire's *Intimate Diaries*: 'As I was crossing the boulevard, rushing a little to avoid the carriages, my halo came loose and fell in the mud of the tarmac. Fortunately I had the time to pick it up again; but then there slipped into my mind a moment later the thought that it boded ill; and since then I have not been able to forget that idea; it didn't give me a moment's rest the whole day long.'

99. *Régnier*: Mathurin Régnier (1573–1613), satirical French poet.

100. *Maurin*: Nicolas-Eustache Maurin (1799–1850). Published a collection of lithographs of famous contemporaries, including doctors.

the time of the uprisings: those of June 1848.

102. *Any Where Out of the World*: the title is taken from Thomas Hood's 'Bridge of Sighs', which Baudelaire translated in 1865. I have respected his spelling of 'anywhere' in two words.

Torneo: Tornea is on the borders of Finland and Sweden. P. S. Hambly has suggested that the mistaken spelling comes from Baudelaire's reading of Toussenel, the Fourierist writer who, in *L'Esprit des bêtes*, described Thornéo [*sic*] as being near the Pole.

103. *Let's Beat up the Poor*: one could compare to this title a statement Baudelaire makes in his article 'The Painter of Modern Life': 'It is philosophy (I'm talking of good philosophy) and religion which order us to care for our poor and infirm relations. Nature (which is nothing other than the voice of interest) commands us to beat them up.'

the eye of a hypnotist could ripen grapes: G. Blin points out that this expression refers to the contemporary practice of using hypnotists to hasten the growth of early fruit. (*Annuaire du Collège de France*, year 66 (1966–7), 485.)

Lélut ... Baillarger: famous doctors of the time who specialized in mental diseases and who had supported the thesis that Socrates had been mad.

104. *a sophist of the Portico*: a Stoic. In Ancient Greece, the philosophers gathered at the Painted Porch or Portico.

105. *Stevens*: Joseph Stevens (1816–92), an animal painter whose painting of 1857, *Intérieur de saltimbanque* (*The Mountebank's Room*), seems to have inspired this prose poem.

... macaroon: the reference is to an incident in Sterne's *Tristram Shandy*.

106. *Roqueplan*: Nestor Roqueplan (1804–70) was a theatre director and critic.

Sainte-Beuve: Charles Augustin Sainte-Beuve (1804–69), in addition to writing poetry and a novel (*Volupté*) the young Baudelaire admired, was the most influential critic of the time.

107. *work without a name*: an allusion to Shakespeare's *Macbeth*, IV. i: Macbeth: 'What is't you do?' All: 'A deed without a name.'

108. *Aretino*: Pietro Aretino (1492–1556), licentious Italian satirist.

109. *Plans and Projects*: these sketches and notes were jotted down in notebooks. They were first published by Baudelaire's friend Nadar.

Catrin: a collaborator of Houssaye, either Louis-Hippolyte Catrin or his son Émile-Nicolas Catrin. Since the latter was born in 1844, the former seems more likely.

110. *Buttes Chaumont*: a rocky outcrop in Paris on which a park has now been built.

Orestes and Pylades: two friends in Greek legend whose names have become proverbial for friendship.

Moloch's altar: supposed Canaanite divinity, to whom, so it is said, human sacrifices were made.

Lazzaronne: lazzarone, to give it its correct spelling: Neapolitan word designating people of the lowest classes.

111. *Hus*: tradition has it that Jean Huss, on seeing a peasant bring a faggot to the stake on which he was to die, cried out: 'O sancta simplicitas!'

112. #: this symbol indicates those poems lightly underlined in the manuscript.

113. *Feuchères (sic)*: Jean-Jacques Feuchère (1807–52), French sculptor.

114. *Musard's garden*: in 1859 Musard had set up a summer concert area in the corner formed by what is now Franklin D. Roosevelt avenue and Cours-la-Reine. It forms the scene for 'The Widows'.

Gray: Thomas Gray (1716–71); English poet, best known for his 'Elegy Written in a Country Churchyard'. Baudelaire paraphrases his lines 'Full many a gem of purest ray serene / The dark unfathomed caves of Ocean bear / Full many a flower is born to blush unseen / And waste its sweetness on the desert air' in the poem called 'Le Guignon' of *Flowers of Evil*.

116. *Boilly*: Louis-Léopold Boilly (1761–1845). The reference is to his painting entitled *The Arrival of the Coach in the Courtyard of the Post-Office*.

Der Tod als Erwürger: the references here are to wood engravings by Alfred Rethel, a German artist much admired by Baudelaire.

THE WORLD'S CLASSICS

A Select List

ORIENTAL TALES
Edited by Robert L. Mack

OVID: Metamorphoses
Translated by A. D. Melville
Introduction and Notes by E. J. Kenney

FRANCESCO PETRARCH:
Selections from the Canzoniere and Other Works
Translated by Mark Musa

EDGAR ALLAN POE: Selected Tales
Edited by Julian Symons

JEAN RACINE: Britannicus, Phaedra, Athaliah
Translated by C. H. Sisson

ANN RADCLIFFE: The Italian
Edited by Frederick Garber

PAUL SALZMAN (Ed.):
An Anthology of Elizabethan Prose Fiction

OLIVE SCHREINER: The Story of an African Farm
Edited by Joseph Bristow

TOBIAS SMOLLETT: The Expedition of Humphry Clinker
Edited by Lewis M. Knapp
Revised by Paul-Gabriel Boucé

STENDHAL: The Red and the Black
Translated by Catherine Slater

ROBERT LOUIS STEVENSON: Kidnapped and Catriona
Edited by Emma Letley

The Strange Case of Dr. Jekyll and Mr. Hyde
and Weir of Hermiston
Edited by Emma Letley

ANTHONY TROLLOPE: The American Senator
Edited by John Halperin

The Last Chronicle of Barset
Edited by Stephen Gill

GIORGIO VASARI: The Lives of the Artists
Translated and Edited by Julia Conaway Bondanella and Peter Bondanella

JULES VERNE: Journey to the Centre of the Earth
Translated and Edited by William Butcher

IZAAK WALTON and CHARLES COTTON:
The Compleat Angler
Edited by John Buxton
Introduction by John Buchan

OSCAR WILDE: Complete Shorter Fiction
Edited by Isobel Murray

A complete list of Oxford Paperbacks, including The World's Classics, OPUS, Past Masters, Oxford Authors, Oxford Shakespeare, and Oxford Paperback Reference, is available in the UK from the Arts and Reference Publicity Department (BH), Oxford University Press, Walton Street, Oxford OX2 6DP.

In the USA, complete lists are available from the Paperbacks Marketing Manager, Oxford University Press, 200 Madison Avenue, New York, NY 10016.

Oxford Paperbacks are available from all good bookshops. In case of difficulty, customers in the UK can order direct from Oxford University Press Bookshop, Freepost, 116 High Street, Oxford, OX1 4BR, enclosing full payment. Please add 10 per cent of published price for postage and packing.